Too Good To Pass By
Up To Date on More Missouri Places
Second Edition

HAVE FUN WITH THESE MISSOURI "VISITS."

Ross Malone

By
Ross Malone

Cover Credit:

Thanks to my good friend John Craig, photographer, of Steelville who took the picture on the cover of this book. It shows the Dillard Mill on the Huzzah River on a warm summer morning. Read about this mill and many others in the section dealing with old grist mills.

www.RossMalone.com

Preface

Some of the places around our state are the sites of things we should never forget. However, with the explosion of modern information, and the seeming nearness of the entire world, we may be missing the unique history that more closely surrounds us. In both the obvious places and those removed from the main roads a perspective awaits the reader which may be forgotten by many. This book looks at those places oft forgotten by the drive-by and fly-over generations.

Of course some of the things are just plain silly. But don't we have room in our lives for a few of the goofy things? I certainly hope so. I truly hope that, as you use this book to plan a few day trips and side trips, or even your Missouri "staycation," you will enjoy yourself as much as I did in preparing the "leads" for you.

Remember, this is not about all of the highly-publicized places that you have probably visited already. This is a compilation of thoughts and opinions about those interesting and less-famous places that surround us. I didn't know until I started preparing this book for publication that I had been driving by two very old grist mills without even recognizing them. What else have I been missing? What have you been missing?

In this book I recommend and suggest several places based on my experiences there. I want the readers to know that none of these establishments have given me samples, money, or any other consideration of any kind. In fact, none of them previously knew that I was thinking of writing about them. My opinions are only that and nothing more.

After reading this book I hope you will think of some other places that should have been included. If you do, will you please let me know? Then when I do a third edition, I'll add those things and give you credit on the "Contributors" page. To contact me, please go to my webpage at www.RossMalone.com. Thanks in advance for your help. I look forward to hearing from you.

Ross W. Malone

Contents

Too Good To Pass By
Up To Date on More Missouri Places

Osceola

Today we think of Osceola as a small town about half way between Kansas City and Springfield. It is at the western edge of the Truman Reservoir and serves as the county seat for St. Clair County. It's interesting and unique history however, began over 200 million years ago.

In what is known as the Mississippian Period a very large meteorite struck the area of Osceola and created a geographical oddity known today as "rock eggs" or more commonly as "round rocks."

"Round Rocks" or "Round Eggs"

These spherical stones were created by the impact and still today are strewn across the countryside. Many of them have been collected in all sizes to adorn lawns and porches and others have found employment as doorstops. For years the area's young people collected them for sale to tourists and now to gardeners.

The area was populated for centuries by Native Americans and was a place where game was plentiful and the fresh waters were full of fish. It was a good home for several nations over the years but, by the time the white man came to record the events of the area, this place was inhabited mostly by the Osage. We will remember 1804 as the year of the Lewis and Clark Expedition but the Osage will remember it as the year when they were ambushed by the Sac at Osceola. Osage canoes were attacked at a bend in the Osage River. In truth, this devastating event was just one of many which were soon to see the great Osage Nation decimated by their rivals.

Known by the Osage as "The Place of Many Swans," this was their home until William Clark and George Sibley convinced them to live adjacent to Fort Osage in present day Jackson County. At one time much of the tribe was drowned in a flash flood and much of their village was destroyed. The Osage determined at that time that they would never again camp with the entire tribe in one place.

They decided that half the tribe would live in the more convenient location down near the river and the rest would live on higher ground. Because of this the two groups came to be known as the Upper Osage and the Lower Osage. A misinterpretation resulted in the groups being called the Greater Osage and the Little Osage as they are referred to in many publications since.

By the 1860s white settlers had discovered this rich area and over 2500 men, women and children were calling the town of Osceola their home. Peace however, had not arrived. Tensions were strong between the residents of Kansas and Missouri and the Kansans had the backing of the federal government. Atrocities were all too common in western Missouri and Osceola was not immune.

On September 22 and 23, 1861 the red-booted Jayhawks from Kansas rode into Osceola and terrorized the town. By the time they left, dozens of Missourians had been killed and the town was a smoking ruin. In two days' time the population dropped from 2500 people to just 200. Other towns were raided across the area at that same time. Most notable among them was Nevada. Nearby Cass County still has a historical area known as "The Burnt District."

This raid on Osceola was later depicted in the novel, *Gone to Texas*, by Forest Walker and then in the opening scene of the movie, *The Outlaw Josie Wales*, starring Clint Eastwood. Two years later when raiders from Missouri attacked Lawrence Kansas, they were said to be shouting, "Remember Osceola!" Today we often hear of "bleeding Kansas" and the sacking of Lawrence but we almost never hear of what led up to that event and how most of the bleeding took place in Missouri.

Now jump forward exactly 150 years and the city council of Osceola has decided to take action. On September 14, 2011, the council members passed a resolution calling on the University of Kansas to drop the Jayhawk as its mascot. Noting that the Jayhawks from Lawrence, Kansas were actually the domestic terrorists of their day, they asked for a change of mascots and an apology from Kansas. Until that should happen the council also asks that all graduates of the University of Missouri shall recognize that Kansas is not a proper place and neither is the university. Therefore kansas and the university of kansas should always be spelled with lower case letters as they are no longer proper nouns.

Downtown Osceola has a quaint look for today's visitors. After the Jayhawks left in 1861 the town slowly grew again but never to its former size. Today the town has less than half the residents it did 150 years ago but the "new" buildings put up mostly in the 1880s are still there and the visual impression of the place is very pleasant. And, of course, any county seat has a certain level of activity and permanence because of the courts and county business being transacted there.

Before leaving the subject of Osceola, this writer wants to recognize who I consider to be the town's most outstanding citizen. Like the town itself, you may not know much about her but in 1805 Dr. Ruth Seevers graduated from Missouri's School of Medicine and began her career of traveling by buggy around Osceola's countryside to care for the ill of St. Clair County. Her method of transportation changed but her dedication did not. For over seventy years (1906-1977) Dr. Seevers served the area and became the oldest practicing female physician in our state!

Devil's Elbow

Someone asked me once which Missouri towns were my favorites. As I thought about that, I realized something. My favorite towns share certain characteristics. First, they are usually river towns. River towns are often picturesque and, because of the flowing water, always changing. Second, my favorite places have a unique quality – often their place in history or a special business or organization. And third, they must have open friendly people. If you know that about me, then you understand why I like Devil's Elbow.

Devil's Elbow got its unique name from its earliest pioneers. The hillsides in the valley of the Big Piney River are covered with native oak trees and these have always held value for anyone wanting to build anything in the Ozarks. This was especially true just before and just after the War Between the States when the railroads were snaking their way westward toward Springfield and the Great Southwest.

The hillsides were swarming with lumberjacks cutting the logs which would become homes, businesses, and railroad ties. In order to get the logs to the main railroad line the easiest way was to float them down the Big Piney to places like Antioch where they could be trimmed, processed and loaded aboard flatcars for their final destinations. This logging process which provided railroad ties gave many pioneers the financial start they needed for success in their new Missouri homes.

But of course, there was a problem. There always is! As the rafts of logs made their way floating down the Big Piney, they reached a sharp bend or "elbow" in the river. This was a spot hated by the lumberjacks because the rafts would often break apart as they rounded the elbow. Because of this, the rafters began to call the place the Devil's Elbow.

Except for the fact that it lay on an old Osage trail between present day St. Louis and Springfield, Devil's Elbow might have faded into history but the trail and the river combined to keep a small population located at or near the place. Just enough of them to merit a post office. When Congress enacted legislation creating a new auto route from Chicago to Los Angeles, Route 66 was born and little Devil's Elbow found itself sitting at one of the few places through the deep Ozarks.

The years brought traffic and the little town was no longer as isolated as it had been. The first road for Route 66 through the town is still marked as a historic byway and provides a scenic and mind-boggling drive. It's mind-boggling because you can imagine cars and even some trucks passing each other as they climbed the hills and hugged the hillsides every day.

Then, as World War II drew nearer, the Army began to build Fort Leonard Wood as a training facility. This fort was to be located on the Ozark Plateau above Devil's Elbow near present day Waynesville and St. Robert. A major problem occurred when the military and commercial trucks tried to take their heavy loads up the narrow curvy roads and steep hills between the river valley and the plateau. The tractor-trailer trucks would often bog down on the grade and additional tractors would be sent to help pull the aircraft and other heavy objects upward.

These trucking problems left many Route 66 motorists stranded for long periods of time in the valley at Devil's Elbow. For some it was a stroke of luck. They had time to discover the beauty of the high limestone bluffs and the cool clear water in the upper Big Piney. There was a wonderful pebble beach that invited swimmers and waders. And there was food.

Big Piney Valley as seen from the Devil's Elbow Bridge

The Munger family recognized the opportunity to turn their barbeque expertise into a profitable venture and opened a small rustic restaurant which actually became a destination all its own. So, stop for a minute and imagine – you're stuck for a short time in a beautiful place with scenery, a beach, nice people and good food. You could do worse!

When Mr. Munger died, his widow married a gentleman named Emmett Moss and the famous Munger Moss Restaurant was born. This Devil's Elbow icon was known up and down "The Nation's Main Street" for its barbeque beef and pork and its blueberry cream pie. Once again, this was not a bad place to be stranded for a while.

Now, Route 66 was not intended to have stranded motorists and the military certainly didn't intend to have problems getting to and from its base so something had to be done about that road at Devil's Elbow. The solution was to cut deep through the limestone hills and create the deepest road cut in North America right there at the Elbow. In addition the little winding road was made straight and had four lanes of divided pavement so the automobiles could pass the lumbering trucks on the hills. These innovations all took place on the other side of the river and now Devil's Elbow was a place that you might or might not see as you whizzed past on this more modern Route 66.

Seeing a bleak future for its hometown, the Munger Moss Restaurant left and opened a new modern brick facility with a motel in Lebanon where this writer grew up relishing the great food which they continued to prepare. Soon Interstate 44 would bypass this facility also but the motel survives to this day as a Route 66 active memory and the restaurant is the office building for Lebanon's Public Schools but the exterior looks the same as it did sixty years ago.

The old original Munger Moss building didn't stay deserted. Today it is known as the Elbow Inn and remains famous for good barbeque and cold beer. It is a friendly place especially for bikers.

Today's visitor to Devil's Elbow will find that the place has not grown but it has modernized. It's near enough to Ft. Wood, Waynesville, and Rolla to make it pleasant and isolated enough to make it even more pleasant. The white limestone bluffs are inspiring and the water of the river is clear, clean and fresh-flowing. The pebble beach and the float-trippers give it character and the old highway bridge provides great views of the Ozark mountain valley. Let's meet at the Elbow Inn for a slab and a cold one!

Gallatin

Gallatin is a prairie town in Northwestern Missouri. It's at the junction of two state highways and all too easy to just breeze right through. If you do, you've missed a connection to some very interesting Missouri history.

This is a railroad town and from the early days that has given it some significance to the area's farmers and merchants. It has attracted various people to the riches from agriculture and from retail commerce. Of course, it's the county seat of Daviess County which contains about 8000 people. It has also been a magnet for the Mormons seeking a safe haven for their practices and was the beginning spot for the Mormon Wars. Today many Mormons make a pilgrimage journey to Gallatin to visit the Adam-Ondi-Ahman community and the nearby sites of the Hans Mill Massacre, and the boomtown turned ghost town, Far West.

It is thought that Frank and Jesse James were the outlaws who, on December 7, 1869, walked into the Daviess County Savings Association in Gallatin, shot the clerk and robbed the bank. At any rate, it was in Gallatin that Frank went on trial in 1883 but was acquitted. Southern sympathizers in this area were not about to hang anyone who struck out against the banks, railroads, or the U.S. Army. Too many Gallatin residents had too recently suffered at the hands of these three groups.

This writer has also found a very different view of the Mormon conflict than ever seen in a history book. If you spend some time in Gallatin, you may get some old timers to share their views on what led to the conflict and why the Governor issued the order to either "expel or exterminate" them.

You may not think of a jail as being a very interesting place but that would probably mean that you haven't yet visited Gallatin. The folks here have always been on the lookout for a way to house the prisoners in a safe, humane, but inexpensive way. It seems that sometimes they just went for two out of those three.

Gallatin's first known jail was called the "pit jail" and it was constructed in 1841. A new stone jail replaced the pit in 1858. The third jail became famous as the "squirrel cage jail" or the "Lazy Susan jail." The interior of this 1887 building actually rotated so that only one cell at a time was exposed to an exit door. It's no longer used but it is still standing for visitors to inspect today.

The Squirrel Cage Jail

People are really the reason why any place is interesting and in the case of Gallatin, there are several important residents who could be considered for mention. There was the outlaw, Johnny Ringo, Governor Alexander Dockery, financial guru – William Thornton Kemper, Sr., and Walter Page, the jazz bassist. However, I like the flamboyant Mrs. Virginia McDonald.

Rising from what might have been her death bed and worried by a family debt of about $8000, she got involved in the family grocery/snack business. Starting with cardboard walls on a blacksmith shop she gradually built a quirky pink and white restaurant with hand-made furnishings and crystal chandeliers. The McDonald family's first meals were hot dogs and hamburgers for the local school children then she expanded to sandwiches and more for Depression era salesmen and business travelers. Word spread and lines formed for the good food at reasonable prices and Virginia's reputation grew.

In time Duncan Hines, Betty Crocker, and others were raving about the meals served there. McDonald's Tea Room, as it was known, was selected as one of the top ten restaurants in the entire nation. Whenever J. C. Penney was back at home in Hamilton, he would always try to get to Gallatin for a meal at Mrs. McDonald's. He would often meet his friend Joyce C. Hall who would drive up from his Hallmark Cards headquarters in Kansas City.

Hall was so impressed by Mrs. McDonald, that he revealed to her his plans for his new Crown Center complex in Kansas City. He told her that he wanted her family to move to Kansas City and be a part of that new Center. McDonald's Tea Room would be the featured restaurant and Virginia McDonald would be a major league restaurateur. Citing the economic impact of her business leaving Gallatin, she refused the offer. Hall offered to place a Hallmark warehouse or some other job creator in Gallatin if she would change her mind. Her loyalty to Gallatin won out and she spent the rest of her life there.

Once, J. C. Penney was invited to leave by Mrs. McDonald because he wasn't wearing a coat and tie. She had her standards and absolutely no one was allowed to break her rules. It was a little bit of a treat afterwards to be welcomed and served in a place where a famous millionaire had been kicked out. By the way, Penney didn't seem to hold a grudge. He remained a regular guest but he was well aware of the rules.

Travelers in the know would often plan their trips to pass through Gallatin so they could stop for a meal in the famous Tea Room. This writer was fortunate enough to dine there before Virginia died. The place was never the same after her departure. The restaurant stayed open under different management for several years but on July 4, 2001 the building and all its contents went up in flames. One final good note about Virginia, her cooking has been preserved in her 1949 wildly popular cookbook which can still be found if you're lucky. (Try the corn muffins.)

Rocheport

Within two decades after Lewis and Clark first made note of this place it was not only becoming settled but the town of Rocheport was chartered. It has never grown large but it has always been interesting. At one point this little port hosted 57 different riverboats making 500 landings per year. They brought manufactured goods to central Missouri and took agricultural products off to the markets.

If you are arriving by way of Interstate 70, I suggest that even before you go to Rocheport, you stop just across the river at the Warm Springs Ranch. This is the beautiful farm that serves as the breeding facility for the Budweiser Clydesdales. The setting is almost as beautiful as the horses. There is a charge for the tour but you might expect that.

Another rural attraction is a working dairy farm that was donated to the University of Missouri by J. C. Penney. The Foremost Dairy Center is run by the university's students and faculty, mostly from the College of Agriculture and the School of Veterinary Medicine. This, being a farm, is not in any town but it is only a few miles east of Rocheport, near Midway.

The Foremost Center has 425 dairy cattle. Most are the black and white Holsteins, but some are the little brown Guernseys that give such rich milk. The tours they give are good and educational for city folk but the farmers who tour the facility do so to catch up on the very latest in dairying. The tours are free and they even let you get your hands dirty if you choose.

If you're in Rocheport, you must visit the Rocheport Museum. There you can learn about Lewis and Clark's "Voyage of Discovery," Missouri River steamboating, the 1840 Whig Convention, Civil War battles, and the Missouri, Kansas and Texas

Railroad, (the KATY Line) built in 1892-1893. Of course this KATY railroad bed is the location of today's very popular KATY Trail for hiking and bicycles.

If you're lucky you can be there for Irish Road Bowling. Yep, bowling right in the middle of the road just north of town. The antique shops are good and plentiful. And then there's the Rocheport General Store.

This is a small store but a nice one. It has a good deli with fairly modest prices. I suggest you try the open face barbeque brisket followed by apple pie with home-made hand-dipped ice cream. It's open from Wednesday through Sunday but why not visit on Friday or Saturday? On those nights they have some good live entertainment. It varies but it's mostly country & folk and frequently blues. They post the entertainment schedule on their webpage so you can plan ahead.

The General Store uses fresh bread baked on the premises daily and I encourage you to purchase a loaf to take with you. You will not be disappointed!

Have you ever driven along going eastward on Interstate 70 and looked around just before you cross the Missouri River west of Columbia? I know you have. You can't help but look at the compelling scenery. Directly in front of you a gigantic green bridge looms and on each side of you is a marshy landscape just full of herons, cranes, geese, mallards, and even some bald eagles. To your right you see the white limestone bluffs that stretch toward Easley. To your left are the huge white limestone bluffs that stretch toward Rocheport. And, atop those bluffs are huge homes.

I have wondered just who might live in those places out in the middle of the state. I have guessed at what the view must be like from there in the morning's light or at sunset. I have thought that, if I ever won the lottery, I would love to have a place there so I could have lunch or dinner while I relish the scenery.

Well, the good news is, you and I do not have to win the lottery to enjoy those places. They're not homes at all – they're parts of the Les Bourgeois Winery. These places are located about one mile north of I-70 and about three miles south of Rocheport on Highway 240. The first place you come to is the new Wine garden and Bistro which offers you wine tasting and dining in an elegant setting with that wonderful view. The next place just a few feet to the north is the old Les Bourgeois tasting room and it's a truly wonderful place.

The old tasting room is now called the A-Frame and it has decks and porches hugging the top of the cliff on six levels. Not six stories but six different levels each separated by three or four steps. This way everyone gets the wonderful view from their own table. From March through October in the A-Frame they offer a picnic basket meal for two for just $7.00 and their own wine by either the bottle or by the glass. Think about this – instead of fast food you can dine like a multi-millionaire for about $20.00 for two!

Marshfield

Marshfield, Missouri was a slow starter. Although settled in 1830, which was kind of early for that part of the country, it just didn't seem to be in much of a hurry to grow. And now, as a bedroom community for many commuters into Springfield, it still seems to be in no hurry. I see that as a very positive thing.

It was the railroad which first boosted the town's growth in 1870. Later it took a longer and steadier spurt of growth as Route 66 came right through town. As traffic on the Mother Road grew, so did Marshfield. When Interstate 44 went north of town, Marshfield didn't roll over and die. The folks made some adjustments and created a newer north side on the town. The result is that the old downtown section still looks much the same as it has for decades. Unlike many by-passed towns, this one has no boarded-up storefronts. Small businesses found a comfortable place to settle on the square around the old courthouse.

One unusual thing in Marshfield is the First Family Library and Museum. It is dedicated to the families who have inhabited the White House. Because of this, 2006 saw the largest gathering of Presidential families in the nation's history take place there. Presidents Harry Truman and George H. W. Bush have also been the guests of this town. The First Family Museum is presently looking for a permanent home but much of the good stuff is on display in the Webster County Museum. Because of the nostalgia associated with Route 66, many famous people have made the drive looking for what remains of the Nation's Main Street. The museum staff can also tell you about these celebrities who stop in town on a regular basis.

Since I'm speaking of Marshfield, I must mention that this was the boyhood home of one of history's greatest astronomers, Edwin Hubble. This man re-wrote everything we thought we knew about the stars. In fact, he showed us that most stars weren't that at all, they were galaxies, each composed of millions of stars. He also showed us that the universe is expanding and he even figured out how to measure the speed of the expansion. Marshfield now has a replica of the famous Hubble Telescope on the courthouse lawn and that section of Interstate Highway 44 has been named The Edwin Hubble Highway.

Having said all this, I should point out that Hubble didn't want to be reminded of his Midwestern roots. He smoked a pipe, wore patches on the elbows of his tweed jackets, and spoke with a phony English accent. The funniest thing is that, while striving to be accepted by the rich and famous, the uppity scientist sought out another Missourian, Walt Disney, for companionship. Disney was always proud of his Missouri background.

Hubble Telescope Replica in Marshfield

Old timers wrote about "the day that Marshfield blew away." They were thinking of April 18, 1880 when an F-4 tornado roared right through the middle of Marshfield and struck many other surrounding counties on the same day. The storm killed 99 residents and injured another 100. That death toll equaled ten percent of Marshfield's population. It also destroyed almost every building in the town. Only fifteen were still standing but many of those were damaged. That is why there are no buildings in Marshfield older than those erected in 1880.

There is another chapter to the story of Marshfield's year of 1880. Less than three months after April's devastation the townsfolk determined that they would not be defeated by an act of nature. They planned a celebration in the face of their losses. Therefore on the Fourth of July, 1880, Marshfield, Missouri staged a parade which has been repeated every year since. It is, in fact, the oldest continuous Independence Day parade in our state or any other state west of the Mississippi.

Independence Day, 1991

Now I want to share a personal thought with you. I can never think of Marshfield without remembering an image of the green trees and white buildings of Marshfield as a background and the blue sky above. Everything else was red, white, and blue. It was July 4, 1991 and President George H. W. Bush was walking the parade route with over a dozen young boys close behind circling on their red, white, and blue decorated bicycles. It showed small-town Mid-America at its most picturesque.

That was then but what about now? Why visit Marshfield today? One reason would come in late April when they have the Cherry Blossom Festival. They have a wonderfully well-rounded set of activities for history buffs and fun lovers alike. Presidential families are a big part of the celebration and so are famous Missourians. They like to say that they focus on the history of the nation and upon the people who shaped it.

Cape Girardeau has its Wall of Famous Missourians along the riverfront, and University City has its Walk of Fame in the Delmar Loop but Marshfield has its Missouri Walk of Fame right there on Clay Street. (One block from the Courthouse Square) During the Cherry Blossom Festival each year Marshfield invites famous Missourians or their descendants to the scene and they install bronze stars into the sidewalks recognizing the accomplishments of that individual. And it's very well done.

So, if you find yourself near Marshfield in April, come on down! And bring your autograph book with you. You never know!

Freebies in St, Louis

Washington, D.C. is known for its many attractions. Since we own them, many are free for us to visit. The city with the second largest number of free attractions happens to be St. Louis. In addition to the free places, there are many that request only a small maintenance fee or donation. Here are some of the good ones.

A world-class **zoo** is housed in Forest Park and admission is $0.00! The **Art Museum** in Forest Park is also absolutely free. Try to find a comparable free museum anywhere. The **Missouri History Museum** in Forest Park is free. Wonderful family-friendly exhibits.

There are always lots of free seats (nearly 1500) at the St. Louis **Municipal Opera (the Muny)** to see musicals on the nation's largest outdoor stage.

<u>Freebies in St. Louis</u> (cont.)

The Jewel Box in Forest Park is free. In fact Forest Park is free. All of St. Louis city and St. Louis County parks are free to the public. Try to find a free park anywhere in the Eastern States.

Walk through the **Laumeier Sculpture Park**. There's no charge. Visit the **Anheuser-Busch Brewery** for free and even get a free beer.

Or visit the animals and shows at **U. S. Grant's Farm** for free – Don't miss the Clydesdales! This is their home. Please be aware that, while this great place is free, it does cost $12.00 to park your car. View the magnificent mosaics at the **Cathedral Basilica** of St. Louis on Lindell Blvd. (Ask why St. Patrick is depicted wearing a red robe.) On some weekday mornings the world renowned **Missouri Botanical Gardens** is free to the public.

Freebies in St, Louis (cont.)

There are some special exhibits which have an admission charge but almost everything at the St. Louis **Science Center** is free. This is a unique place for families. The World Bird Sanctuary is a unique walk-through experience and next door is the **Lone Elk Park** where you can have up-close-and-personal encounters with bison, elk, and others as you drive your car through for free.

Even the **Gateway Arch** is free. You have to pay to ride to the top but there is plenty to do at ground level. I haven't even mentioned the festivals and special events or the places with very small fees. Why not start with the free ones for now?

Freebies in St, Louis (cont.)

If you happen to be a history buff, stop at any book store or museum shop and purchase a guide book to the area's statues, historic homes, or cemeteries. You will not believe who is buried in the two oldest cemeteries! These places provide a nice quiet walk and some jaw-dropping discoveries. Bring your camera! On a personal note, I would not go walking in the wonderful old cemeteries by myself. For safety's sake, I would take a guided tour or at least tag along as part of a group.

Vintage Baseball is free for spectators and a very pleasant way to spend an afternoon. Read more about this later in this book. Bring lawn chairs.

<u>Weingarten</u>

As you breeze along Highway 32 between Ste. Genevieve and Farmington you will see a little hamlet named Weingarten. It's no surprise to see a German name in this place where everything has an early French or early German origin. With those two nationalities present it's also logical to see a place whose name means Wine Garden. These hills are full of vineyards and good local wine is produced in many nearby wineries.

This community has one church (with a surprising membership of 655) and a handful of houses and one business. But nearby is a fireplace chimney which is the only remaining clue to a fascinating chapter of the town's history. This fireplace was the nicest part of the Officer's Quarters for the Americans who operated a World War II P.O.W. camp in this quiet farm country. There were thirty of these camps in Missouri alone during the war years.

The government began buying up land in the summer of 1942, the American soldiers moved in and they were soon followed by Italian prisoners. That's right, they were all Italian. No one wanted to bring Germans into this German-American population. By the time camp operations were in full swing, the facility covered 835 acres, had 1,500 American soldiers, a large civilian staff, and 3,500 prisoners. So the little town of 133 people today temporarily had a population of over 5,000.

In his informative book, *The Enemy Among Us*, David Fiedler, quotes a farmer's wife at Weingarten laughing at the irony of the situation. Mrs. Henry Harter said her son, Austin, was in Alaska, "…keeping a lookout for the Japanese while Japanese are to be moved into our pasture." In the end however, no Japanese were brought to Weingarten.

The physical facility had the barracks, mess halls, and yard areas that you might expect. It also had five deep wells, a sewage system, and a tall water tower to create water pressure. The whole place was surrounded by twelve guard towers. If this sounds pretty bleak, then you might be surprised.

By all accounts the prisoners were treated well. They were comfortable and the food was good. Compared to the battlefield conditions from which they were extricated, this was pretty good. There were some "hard cases." Some of Mussolini's Black Shirts were in the camp. They were not so cooperative and were often isolated from the others and were the subject of additional security. Even so, two of them escaped one day. They were soon picked up in Ste. Genevieve. I don't know where they thought they could go. Maybe they weren't told that they were in the middle of the continent.

Many of the prisoners from Weingarten and the other camps were allowed to leave on escorted trips to help with planting, harvesting, putting up hay, and the other farm duties. They were paid 80 cents per day and they covered the gap created by all of the American boys being at war. Some prisoners even went into the towns and helped the local merchants to operate their businesses.

The day came when Allied forces took over Italy and the Italian people had disposed of their dictator and joined the fight against the Nazis. At this time many of the prisoners joined all-Italian regiments and went back to Europe to fight on our side. Others remained until the end of the war at which time they were sent back to their homeland.

It's interesting that, when seeing the destruction from the fierce fighting throughout Italy, some of them remembered the beautiful countryside, the friendly people, and the peace they had witnessed in Ste. Genevieve County. Many of these P.O.W. soldiers actually returned to Missouri and settled into new lives.

Another interesting group of prisoners were identified by their captors as being bright and possessing leadership qualities. These men were given special training and education to prepare them for post-war Italy. They were to be the seeds of Democracy and the new leaders of their communities. They were to be our new friends and allies in the years to come.

So, what became of Camp Weingarten? Immediately at the conclusion of the war the facilities were torn down and the land was sold back to area farmers. It's now covered with corn, soybeans, grapes, and memories. You just never know what memories are contained in a tiny town and the farm fields around it!

Blackwater

. How many times have you been to Arrow Rock? It seems the perfect little town to visit. It has history, quaint buildings, and friendly informed people who are extremely proud of their town. But don't be in too much of a hurry to get there! Between the interstate and Arrow Rock there is another small town brimming with history, quaint buildings, and community pride. Have you been to Blackwater?

Right there by the Blackwater River is a pretty little railroad town where gardeners are at work every morning tending to rock gardens and flowerbeds and gigantic sidewalk potted trees and flowers. Yes some of these are on private property but many of the flower gardens are on public land and are so well-maintained just because Blackwater people appreciate aesthetics.

Have you ever tried to find a clean public restroom when you're away from home? Good luck with that! Now, in Blackwater they have signs pointing the way behind the old-fashioned "calaboose" to some restrooms that are worth seeing even if you don't need to. Clean and cute, they say hospitality in a way nothing else can.

To get to these restrooms, or anything else for that matter, you have to go past the windmill right in the middle of the town's main intersection. The framework of the old structure is covered with hanging flowers and water slowly drips downward keeping them irrigated. There's a constant wet spot in the street underneath but that's a small price to pay for the old-fashioned charm of the thing.

Do you like live theater? This tiny town has it. How about good food? Choose between two distinct restaurants both on the main street. One is a typical small town storefront café with Formica décor, casual comfort food, and pleasant conversation. The other is a little more formal dining room in the hotel across the street. The hotel is next to the railroad station so its restaurant is called the Iron Horse. It is staffed by some very accomplished people who mix fine dining with Midwestern casual for a culinary treat.

If you're lucky, you might stumble across another little eatery that is unique and very charming. Because of the advanced age of the operator, this one may not be doing business in the near future. There is no menu. You just take whatever is being dished out. It's often chili or soup along with some delightful sides. The real treat is the home-made pies.

Don't miss these. To find this place, you will need to ask the locals. It's hiding in plain sight.

Be warned that except for the restaurants, nothing here opens before 10:00 AM. At least that's what the signs all tell us. However, if you find a business open before 10:30, mark that on your calendar. It's a rare event. If you're antiquing, it's worth the wait and two of the shops are outstanding. Anywhere on the main street is a pleasant place to sit and spend some time. You will want to be sure and notice the interesting buildings including the Independent Telephone Museum and the City Hall. Both are very old and special.

Many visitors to Blackwater have gone straight to the Bucksnort Trading Post. It's a wonderful place but they have moved to a new location at the west end of Arrow Rock.

Blackwater is a genuine small town with an appreciation of its own history as a part of America's westward movement. The merchants are entrepreneurs who have recognized the special appeal of the place and are making a living from it. The flowers are not tended by teams of paid horticulturists but by local residents with a flair for creating something special. It's just a place that's too darned nice to keep driving past.

Potosi

Everyone knows Potosi. When you're driving to Trout Lodge, or Mark Twain National Forest, or Lake Wapapello, you'll probably pass through Potosi. Maybe you shouldn't pass through. Maybe you should plan to stop for a bit. Potosi has fast food and good food – take your choice. As with many small towns, you might want to ask some locals about their favorite place to eat. In small restaurants, when a particular cook moves, the quality of the meals moves right along with him or her.

Potosi is surrounded by a bounty of natural interests and history. But the town itself is something quite unique in our state's history. Did you know for instance, that Potosi was the first real Missouri town to be established away from a river? All of our early towns grew up on the banks of the Mississippi and then the Missouri River. Waterways were the highways of the past. They were the only connection that existed between those early communities. Then came Potosi.

In about 1770 a mining operation began in the area and it was called *Mine au Breton*, because its founder, Francis Azor, was a Frenchman from Brittany. One story says that "The Breton" and a hunting partner were following a bear when they discovered a huge exposed section of lead ore on the ground. Another tale is that the two stopped and built a campfire by a large tree root which then melted from the heat of the fire. It was a vein of lead. Today Jefferson Street in Potosi where these events occurred is called "Bearfoot" by the locals.

Then in 1798, Moses Austin was granted land by the Spanish Government and he brought his family here to lay out the plot for a new town. This was done on 40 acres of his own land which he donated for a county seat. He named it for the great mining center in Bolivia called Potosi. Where "The Breton" had just taken ore from the top of the ground, Austin began to tunnel into the ground for the ore and built smelters and other equipment for a serious mining operation. He also opened a store where he was known for fairness in his pricing. His son, Stephen, grew up here in this mining town where he played in the streets and yards with the miner's children as well as the Indian children who still lived in the area and came to Austin's store to trade.

People in eastern Missouri will recognize the names of two other prominent Potosi residents from those early days. James Bryan and Firmin Desloge both made their marks on our history and our commerce. Of course Desloge, Missouri is named for the later gentleman.

Although the Osage were frequent visitors to Potosi, relations with them were not always good. In 1802 they had attacked the settlement in force. After that time, relations improved between the Osage and the miners. But this event also gave the men of the community a reputation as Indian fighters. During these years Moses' son Stephen continued to mature and showed some of his father's leadership abilities. He was elected to serve as a Representative in the State Legislature.

Potosi continued to grow and on August 12, 1816, the very first Presbyterian Church in Missouri was founded in Potosi. (Today Moses Austin's tomb is located at this church.)

In 1821 Moses Austin did a very remarkable thing. He packed up some supplies and left Potosi, crossed the great desert of the southwest and continued right on out of the country. He traveled all the way to Mexico City where he requested an audience with the Emperor. And he got it! Can you imagine someone hitchhiking today from a little woodland town in Canada to Washington, D.C. and asking to speak to the President? It was an amazing thing and he pulled it off.

Austin asked for Mexico to grant great areas of land in Texas to the people of Potosi and the surrounding area if they would settle there. Mexico was having trouble controlling the Indian Nations in such a large area but the Potosi men were known to be a rough, tough bunch who could take care of themselves when it came to Indians. The Emperor agreed and Moses returned home to tell the news and lead the Missouri pilgrims to Texas.

There is a lot more to the story but the basic facts are that Moses became ill on the way home and died shortly after arriving. So, under the law of the day, his son, Stephen, was obligated to hold up his father's end of the bargain. Thus Stephen Austin led the group and became known as "The Father of Texas."

Another facet of this story took place in 1938. In that year Potosi went to battle with Texas (in court of course) over the bodies of Moses Austin and his wife. Texas wanted them removed to a shrine in the Lone Star State. Potosi won that legal battle and Moses Austin remains buried today under his monument behind the Presbyterian Church in the town he founded.

Moses Austin Grave and Memorial

Photo by Deanna Mercille

A fierce tornado swept through town on December 21, 1967 and destroyed the City Hall and several businesses. Today you can't tell that the destruction ever occurred. Potosi is a resilient place.

This information only scratches the surface of the history of Potosi and the early families. Why don't you do a little mining of your own for information and then visit the place. They'll make you welcome.

Missourians Travel the World
(Without Leaving Home)

There was a time when people across the frontier were choosing names for their new communities and they wanted them to have the sound of importance and permanence. So they would choose names of heroes around the world like Hannibal, Hermann, Atlas, Augusta, Bolivar, or the many saints.

One of my favorite places lies along the south side of the Missouri River in Lafayette (There's another one!) County. Right on Highway 24 lies the small town of Napoleon. Go east on 24 for just five miles and you're in the town of Wellington. That's pretty good but can you guess what little community lies right between them? Of course it's Waterloo. The residents of the area tell me that there was no plan to do this. "It's just a coincidence." they say. Maybe.

There are many named for historic kingdoms and an astounding number named for trails, riverboats and railroads. Some places are named for national heroes such as Washington, Jefferson, Franklin, Lewis, Clark, Kearney, Jackson, Rolla (Raleigh), Boone, or Hamilton. Still more honor cities of the world with romantic sounding names such as Alexandria, Warsaw, Amsterdam, Glasgow, Memphis, Milan, Madrid, Montreal, Hamburg, Cabool (an archaic spelling of Kabul) London, or Rome.

Then there are those far away countries with strange-sounding names. At least the residents of those countries would think so. Japan (JAY-pan in Missouri) , Cuba (KEW-ba in Missouri), Lebanon (LEB-nun here), Paris (We say PAR-is), Hayti (Haiti) (In Missouri we say HAY-tie). How many of these Missouri foreign places have you visited so far?

__Monett__

You might describe Monett as an in-between place. It's sort of in-between Joplin, and Springfield, and Branson. Its closest neighbors include Pierce City, Verona and Purdy. With a population of almost 9,000 it sits right on the Barry-Lawrence County line. So, if it's neither here nor there, why is it so significant?

My answer to that would be that the people of Monett have always been so independent. Free thinkers often make for interesting history so I'll share some of the events in Monett's growth and you see if you don't agree with me.

On July 3, 1910 the Holbrook Helicopter Aeroplane group of Monett and Joplin built a strange aluminum combination of airplane and helicopter. It flew at an altitude of about 5 feet for about 6 minutes on this day. This was a half-century before small helicopters began being used in the Korean War! That's right – just after the Wright Brothers got off the ground for the first time, the folks in Monett were building aluminum helicopters that actually flew and hovered!

On April 28, 1911 Monett expected to be "flying high" according to the *Monett Times*. They were pinning their hopes on the new airplane industry and the Monett Aeroplane Company. The paper stated, "…a smart start here will no doubt develop into an immense industry in a few years." Of course it didn't develop into an immense industry there but how innovative these people were and what a unique place in history!

On June 30 of that same year the *Monett Times* stated, "If you fail to attend our Fourth of July celebration next Tuesday you will ever regret it." Does that sound like a threat? They were expecting crowds of people to come and see the new aeroplanes. Sure enough photos show the 4th of July celebration brought thousands of people to the airfield to see these new machines.

To tell the whole story, we must remember that some of the investors and supporters in this aviation enterprise were from Joplin and a true aviation pioneer, Hugh A. Robinson was doing his thing a few miles away in Neosho. This was truly a greenhouse for the seeds of the airplane industry. Even though the Monett helicopter was constructed with aluminum tubing, it and the wooden stick airplanes were just basically kites with motors. All their surfaces were covered with cloth then painted with lacquer to give them strength and body.

One of the area pilots found himself high in the air when his engine died. He walked on the framework of the plane and kept it balanced until it could glide to the ground. Oh yes, I should mention that his day job was as a circus acrobat. Those magnificent men in their flying machines were awesome! And while Monett, may be an in-between sort of place right now, it was once the very center of some wonderful ingenuity, enterprise, and daring.

If you ask a local about the town's history, you will probably get an earful about the baseball and football teams. The best of the bunch may have been the Monett Athletics semi-pro baseball team. In 1910 they opened the season with an exhibition game against the St. Louis Browns. (Of course this Browns team was a big league team in the American League.) After losing that game, the team went on to a record of 54-7. They followed that with another good year in 1911.

Ticket prices ranged from 10-25 cents and hundreds of people showed up for the games. The team's following was so big that when they traveled to out-of-town games, the Frisco Railroad would arrange for special trains to carry the fans.

In time the team had trouble paying the players and paying the rent so they went out of business but just think about this – In 1910 and 1911 Monett had a wonderful baseball team and all of the excitement of the new aviation industry. Life must have been truly fun in Monett where even the sky wasn't the limit.

Finally let me make a shameless plug for another of my books. *The Monett Nine* is a piece of very accurate historical fiction. It's written for young readers from 10-14 years old but a lot of adults have enjoyed it too. It's an adventure story that gives a lot of details about life in a small Ozarks town more than a century ago. It's in most Missouri libraries. If not in yours, just make a request.

Dutzow

Dutzow? What is a Dutzow? It's a tiny place in Warren County which gave birth to much of what makes Missouri unique – that's what! This story of Dutzow begins with the second of its most influential citizens. Gottfried Duden only lived there for three years but just think about what he set in motion.

In 1824 Duden established a farm just north of the Missouri River. In 1827 he left and went back to Germany. In the meantime he wrote letters home describing the Missouri River Valley as a wonderful place comparable to the Rhine Valley in the Deutschland. Except, according to Duden, it didn't have all the political woes of Germany. His glowing reports caused tens of thousands of Germans to flood into the length of the Missouri River Valley during the next three decades. These German immigrants are known by some as the "followers of Duden."

While that was significant enough, there were ripples that followed the initial plunge into the American pool.

Germany at the time was the world's leader in education, philosophy, agriculture and commerce. These immigrants may have settled in log cabins but just until they could quickly erect substantial homes of stone and brick. They were here to stay. They were here to improve everything. Soon the entire Missouri Valley was lined with stores, farms, vineyards, factories, and Turner Halls.

These Turner Halls were places of self-improvement and social activity. Gymnastics, music, riflery, theater, poetry, and other classes abounded. Even marching classes were offered. When the War Between the States broke out, Northern Generals in Missouri found men who already could march and shoot as well as most soldiers of the world. In fact many of Missouri's fighting units were organized at the Turner Halls and the German churches across central Missouri.

And speaking of Churches, many of the beautiful churches in the valley were built by the stonemasons and bricklayers who followed Duden to "The New Rhine." As you approach Dutzow from any direction you will see Catholic Churches, and Lutheran Churches, and others that began as German Evangelical Churches and German Reformed Churches. Those latter two denominations first merged together then joined with the Congregational Churches of New England's Pilgrims. They are now known as the United Church of Christ. These U.C.C. churches are everywhere around Dutzow and are as plentiful as their Catholic brethren.

To train ministers, these early Germans next purchased some land near Dutzow (and Marthasville) and started the Eden Theological Seminary. This seminary later moved to Webster Groves and trains ministers for several denominations. At Eden's old site the beautiful campus was reborn as Emmaus Home was created to care for adults who are mentally unable to live independently.

One of the main reasons people find themselves driving through Dutzow is in search of fine Missouri wine. This is the heart of Missouri's Wine Country. The Blumenhof Vineyards operate one of the larger wineries in the area and many others, both larger and smaller, are nearby.

Just across the farm fields to the west of Dutzow is a large stream, Charrette Creek, which enters the Missouri nearby. This was the site of a small fort and seven houses when Lewis and Clark came through in 1804. It was the last outpost of European civilization they were to see. On their return in 1806 the expedition's men spotted a cow in a field here and knew that they must be near a settlement. They shot rifles and shouted into the air in joy on knowing that they were back home. Two young Scotsmen who were visiting the village prepared "a most agreeable meal" for the returning heroes.

Even with all my talk of Gottfried Duden, I haven't mentioned this place's most famous and important residents. The family of Daniel Boone lived a stone's throw northeast of town as did their son, Nathan, and many friends who came here with them. The grave monument for Daniel and Rebecca is just northwest of Dutzow. (Nearer to Marthasville.)

The Boone's Bones

A time came when Kentucky demanded the return of the bodies of Daniel and Rebecca Boone but the families pointed out that Daniel held a good deal of contempt for Kentucky and said he never wanted to go there again. But, when the courts finished with the matter, it was ordered that their remains be dug up and sent back to the bluegrass state.

A story is told that the family members pointed out the graves of two slaves who were buried next to the Boone's and it is they (the slaves) who now lie under the monument in Kentucky. Others deny that completely.

However, forensic anthropologists in 1983 said that the bones in Kentucky do not belong to the Boone family. At any rate, the visitors' book at the monument in Missouri shows people from all over the western world stopping to visit the large granite boulder honoring Warren County's most famous residents.

A wealthy family which is mindful of history has purchased the farm where Daniel and Rebecca Boone died. At that time it was the home of their adopted son, David Bryan. This family is doing a great deal to preserve and enhance the property. At times now it hosts special events but one day soon, it will probably be a tourist attraction in its own right. The property is known as the Boone Monument Farm.

We can't leave Dutzow without mention of The Kansas, Missouri, & Texas Railroad. As their trains whizzed along tracks on the north side of the great river, the china service, the walls, and other items were decorated with images of a kitty named KATY. This name was derived from the initials of the railroad. Eventually the KATY line went defunct and nothing remained but the tracks and rail bed. Now the tracks have be removed and re-cycled and the bed has been rebuilt providing a bicycle trail across the entire state.

This Katy Trail takes cyclists past towering limestone bluffs and beside the river and bottomland fields and many pleasant little places to stop. Dutzow is one of the best of those. Bikers are invited to stop and rest and maybe purchase some refreshments. In fact, many people who don't have bikes or a good way to transport them, go to Dutzow to rent bikes for the day.

This little place has a recorded history going back well over 200 years and has known the flags of Spain, France, England, and the United States. It's amazing to realize that while the Boones did settle down here, many people like Duden, Lewis & Clark, and today's cyclists have been just passing through. As with the residents of Fort Charrette, the folks who live here make passing through a very pleasant experience.

Weston

There was a time when the western edge of Missouri was a straight line including Joplin, Kansas City, and points eastward. Places like Maryville and St. Joseph were not in Missouri. Then came the Platte Purchase which moved our western border over to the banks of the Missouri River. And that's how Weston and many other communities came into our state. Weston was the oldest community in the Platte Purchase and being the farthest west of any community at that time is was called West Town.

This may have been even more significant in those days than now. You see, as late as 1850 there were more than 300 steamboats docking at the Port of Weston every year. Only St. Louis was a larger and busier inland port. With 5000 residents, this West Town was larger than either Kansas City or St. Joseph. Weston did, in fact, enjoy being called "The Queen of the Platte Purchase."

While talking about this period in Weston's history we don't want to overlook an earlier time when the Louis and Clark

Expedition was here. They camped for a time at a spot near where the Town Hall now stands. They wrote in their journals about a sweet clear spring near the present town.

Flooding has always been a problem for Weston and they had some major fires but nothing compared to the toll taken by the War Between the States which included the battles and skirmishes between Missourians and their neighbors in Kansas. Weston was devastated and the population fell to about 1000. Even now, it's only about 2000.

The early prosperity of the town resulted in the well-constructed and ornate buildings which greet visitors today. Also, Weston escaped much of the burning and destruction at the hands of the Jayhawks and the US Army which destroyed too many other Missouri communities. As a result of these early buildings surviving, in 1972 much of the town was declared to be a Historic District and placed on the National Registry of Historic Places. This includes picturesque businesses and residences.

But, I'm not suggesting that you visit Weston 150 years ago. I'm saying that you will have a great time visiting Weston right now. Here are some amazing things to see and do. If you're young or if you like live Irish music, you must spend some time on Friday, Saturday, or Sunday at O'Malley's Pub.

You've heard of Irish pubs before and true, they usually are fun but this one is something so very special! Founded in 1842, it is the oldest brewery west of the Hudson River. They brew O'Malley's Emerald Lager, O'Malley's I.S.B. (Irish Style Bitter Ale), O'Malley's Irish Cream Ale, and a dark brown Irish-style ale known as O'Malley's Festival Ale. And, yes, this is all served in a large, old, two-story, open building with a stage for live Irish music! And they have a full bar with unique mixed drinks too.

Several decades ago I was introduced to McCormick Whiskey. This smooth whiskey has a truly interesting heritage. In 1804 Lewis and Clark discovered a sweet water spring at the foot of limestone bluffs. Later Ben Holladay recognized this as the perfect place to provide an answer for the wagon trains seeking fresh water and good whiskey. In 1856 he began distilling. This rich but smooth Missouri-made product sells for a fraction of what some distillers charge for similar products. The distillery is just outside the town on the south side but they maintain a nice store and a sampling bar in the middle of town. This business, originally known as the Holladay Distillery, has been operating continuously at the same location longer than any other distillery in the United States.

Speaking of Ben Holladay, he was known to most of the world as "The Stagecoach King." After being a businessman in Weston he took a huge leap and started a stage operation known as the Overland Stage Company which he sold in 1866 for 1.5 million dollars. From there he went on into further ventures in transportation. While he was an important businessman, he was quite a terrible person on the personal level. I'll leave that for you to look up if you're interested.

Now, with good local wineries, a relaxing state park, several Bed & Breakfast establishments, and all of the things mentioned above, you would probably enjoy spending some time here. Buffalo Bill Cody and four generations of Daniel Boone's family certainly did! In fact, one national publication selected Weston as one of the 100 nicest small towns in America.

This writer's favorite little spot in Weston is at a fountain right on the main street. The little fountain sends out streams so people can always find a refreshing sip of cool water at any time. The water which is not used by people falls downward into basins around the bottom of the fountain and is perfect for watering your horses or mules. It's both pretty and functional – just like this neat little town.

Steelville

One of my favorite small towns seems like it would be right in the middle of everything but you actually have to do some driving just to get there. Let me clarify and say the Steelville really is in the middle of everything – It was recently the population center of the United States. It's just a few picturesque miles south of I-44 and a little east of Rolla.

I used to love reading my National Geographic magazines each month because they always seemed to show the most interesting places and people. They always made me want to visit those places. I was really excited one day when my new magazine arrived with an article featuring Steelville. That's the day I dropped my subscription. I don't understand why the writer did a hit job on this neat place but, for some strange reason, he did the only negative article I had ever seen in that publication. People who know Steelville still bristle at the mention of that condescending article.

Let's talk a little about why Steelville is one of my favorite places. First, this area was chosen as a part of the National Scenic Riverways because it really is <u>scenic</u>. This beautiful area attracts huge numbers of float trippers every year because of its clean fresh rivers and its natural beauty. Why go camping or canoeing here? Because it's a beautiful place in the Ozark hills. Important streams in the area include the Meramec River and two spring fed creeks, the Yadkin and Whittenburg. Just to the east a few miles are the Huzzah and Courtois.

Steelville has twice been destroyed and twice rebuilt. The first disaster was in 1898 when a flood ravaged the town killing many and sweeping most of the place away. The other time was only six years later, in 1904, when a fire destroyed almost the entire town. In both cases, the citizens rebuilt and early in the last century, the entire town took on a project to spruce the place up and give it much of what we see today.

The Meramec Music Theater is a surprisingly large operation for a town of only 1400. It features local people and brings in acts from other places on a regular basis. One thing you'll notice about this place is that people here don't take themselves too seriously. They're all about having a good time and that makes for a good place to visit.

Antiquing is also good in Steeleville and this writer enjoys finding good quality walnut furniture here. I've always found the shop owners to be both honest and fair. In fact, fairness seems to be a true characteristic of the population. When I lived in Farmington and traveled through Steelville regularly on my way to visit my family in Springfield, I could always count on good food at a reasonable price. When my mother's car broke down near Steelville, she got it to a local mechanic who did a great job, provided her with a comfortable waiting room, and charged her a very small amount. It would have been easy to charge her more but, as I said, fairness seems to be a characteristic of the population.

A good closing thought is the town's own motto: "Steelville, Missouri – where the rivers come together – where the people come together!"

Washington

As I constantly travel around the state, people ask where I live, and they never understand what I tell them. I live on a hilltop in Franklin County between Union and Washington. What county? Where are those places? Well, if you don't know – you really should!

Washington has 445 buildings listed on the National Register of Historic Places. That's more than any other community in Missouri. It's also the home of the Town and Country Fair. That's the state's third largest after the State Fair and the Ozark Empire Fair. It's also in the center of Missouri's Wine Country with dozens of wineries on the hillsides sloping toward the Missouri River.

In the earliest days an Osage village stood where the town's large Mercy Hospital stands today. French trappers were working the local streams prior to 1804. Lewis and Clark were here that year. Daniel and Nathan Boone's family and friends were among the earliest settlers. Within a very short time a riverboat landing grew up on the site and, in the 1820s, the new town of Washington was platted. By 1832 the Germans were arriving.

The arrival of Germans was very important because these industrious settlers were all about permanence. Their homes and commercial buildings were built not of wood but of brick. The town at that time came to be known as "The Brick Town of Missouri." In 1854 John B. Busch, older brother of St. Louis's Aldolphus Busch, started his brewery in Washington and, even today, it is one of the most beautiful old buildings in the city.

At this time in the world's history Germany led the world in science, medicine, art, and philosophy. The immigrant Germans brought industry, commerce, education, and more to this part of the state. They identified more closely with the cities, industry, and banking of the North as opposed to the rural and agrarian society of the South. They also brought anti-slavery feelings which would become increasingly important as the nation headed toward war.

Some of the earliest industries involved brewing and fermenting alcoholic drink but there were other things also. Zithers were extremely popular musical instruments of the day and the best zithers in the world came from Washington. Then there was, and still is, the manufacture of corncob pipes. These "Missouri Meerschaums" are lined with just the right amount of clay to keep the bowl from burning but they still dispel heat and deliver the user a nice cool smoke.

I could literally write a book about the interesting history of Washington, Missouri but lots of people have already done that. You see, this place is loaded with some of the best historians anywhere. Missouri certainly has some of the finest professional historians at its major institutions like museums and universities but it also has some fine amateurs. Among those, Washington may be in a class by itself. People like Leroy Danz and Ralph Gregory have been leaders of dozens of dedicated people in the area's six historical societies and the Four Rivers Genealogical Society.

So when you visit Washington, be certain to allow time for the three museums operated by the Washington Historical Society. If you have ancestors from this area, be sure to avail yourself of the contents of the Kiel File. It is a genealogy tool which may be unique in all the world.

Washington may have the oldest brass band in the state and west of the Mississippi but they are unable to document an exact starting date so the Municipal Band at El Dorado Springs has that honor for now. At any rate, this fine band offers free concerts at the Riverfront Park and at local wineries all through the warm weather. If you attend a concert, say hello to the tuba player. I'll be happy to meet you.

The two highways serving Washington meet south of town in a big intersection with seven traffic lanes in each direction. The intersection is full of big box stores and fast food joints clambering for you attention and your money. Sadly that is the impression that too many folks have of this picturesque and historic town. Visitors must go a few blocks north toward the riverfront and experience the old town with its farmers market, coffee shops, antiques, cafes, and other businesses. When locals saw the steel I-beams going up for the Bank of Washington's new four-story building they worried that it would spoil the atmosphere of the old town. But care was taken to match architecture of the stores and churches so the town retains its inviting charm.

Across the street from the bank is Missouri's finest artist (in this writer's opinion) and he works regularly there in his local studio. Gary Lucy's Gallery is a working shop where you can often meet the artist and where the city's mayor (Sandy Lucy) is always happy to discuss the paintings and answer questions about her town. She will, no doubt, refer you to the visitors center on the river front one block away.

In addition to the fine dining at local restaurants, some folks make a point to visit Wimpy's and order a brain sandwich. The town also has two fine butcher shops which still show the German influence in their offerings. Raw Hack draws many people to these meat cutters but the important thing for me is that they use locally-raised beef and pork with no feed lot cattle at all.

In an earlier paragraph I mentioned the two highways leading into town but you might also like to arrive by boat at the town's nice dock. Better for most people would be to ride the Amtrak train right to the visitor's center on the riverfront. Some of the best cafes, Bed & Breakfasts, antiques, and shops are within a block or two of the train. There is also a very nice riverfront park and a walking trail starting from there. The Katy Trail is just across the Missouri River Bridge.

So, here's your plan. By train, boat, or car, arrive in Washington with plenty of time for a pleasant stroll, some shopping, a good meal, and a free concert on the Mighty Missouri. Then either a nice hotel or a pleasant ride home. That's a good day's recipe!

AUTHOR'S WISH LIST

As I drive around our state,

I can't help but notice that many small businesses are either struggling or gone completely. This is not completely due to the economy or what some people consider to be the evil Walmart.

Sometimes it's due to poor management.

Hannibal contains good examples of this.

The city has done a wonderful job of blending the tourist attractions, convenient parking, and modern amenities. However, the merchants have been spoiled by their unique circumstance. They expect the tourists to flow in and flood the town with money. Some seem to have forgotten that their job is to <u>serve</u> those moneyed tourists. In Hannibal and similar places a guest is too often greeted by greasy-haired tattooed young men who feel that your presence will somehow slow down the clock until they can leave. Or the young women who resent the customers because they might interfere with the gossiping or the texting which goes on continually.

Hannibal: (Continued)

I have to admit that I have often left a business with a smile on my face and saying to myself, "What a crusty old guy that was!" We have all enjoyed the bossy old lady who runs her shop with a no-nonsense iron hand. I truly enjoy a colorful character but I truly resent a rude clerk of any age who expects me to purchase his goods or services when he tries so hard to make my experience in his place unpleasant.

And for many clerks, restaurateurs, and shop owners, two words: Eye Contact. Stop ignoring your customers! Restaurant manages, listen to me. I understand that you train your servers to be attentive. Good. But I wish they would not pester me while I eat. Filling my coffee cup and checking in with me is not the same thing as interrupting my conversation six or eight times to ask, "Is everything OK?" Many merchants in many towns spend a lot of money advertising to get us in the door then treat us rudely when we arrive. This is a balancing act that good entrepreneurs can manage and master.

There's an Antique Mall east of Columbia that deserves special mention. I challenge you to walk into that place with a smile on your face and still be smiling when you leave. I don't think it can be done

Ste. Genevieve:

Ste. Genevieve, like many other towns, needs to spruce up. I hate to mention this because the citizens of Ste. Gen. have, for generations, done an outstanding job of keeping their unique history alive. But when I lived in Ste. Genevieve County I was in town often and I speak from experience. This is not a wealthy town but it doesn't need to look shabby either. I wish the local government and civic organizations would do more to dress the place up and make it more inviting.

I would suggest that the civic leaders take a road trip and visit such places as Weston, Arrow Rock, Blackwater, or Washington. Plantings, banners flying, and paint go a long way to making a town a memorable place. And don't you love those directional signs that some towns have to help us find our destinations? Other historic towns have learned that careful development in historic districts is a pain in the neck but well worth the trouble in the long run. Plans are well under way at this time to develop a formal historic district in Ste. Gen. This would be a good time to start a local overhaul.

Have you ever been to a mall and noticed all of the men sitting in the lobby areas while their wives and girlfriends shop? Of course you have. Have you ever noticed how many malls provide benches or comfortable seating for people to collect themselves, meet up, or enjoy an ice cream cone? Many towns really should keep this in mind if they hope to be more attractive to visitors. A few well-placed, all-weather benches are inviting to people of all ages. Older people who need a rest, younger people who need to feed the baby, and children who need a "time out" all profit from a relaxing shady or sunny bench. A little brass plaque on a bench even provides good advertising for local businesses and civic clubs. The "Man's Land" described later in Hamilton, Missouri is a wonderful example of this concept done right.

Springfield:

Even though I own property in **Springfield** and spend a good deal of time there, I try to avoid spending money there. The reason is that many of Springfield's merchants have discount cards for the local residents. The effect is that they pay one price but you and I, as visitors, pay a higher price for the same merchandise. They make a better profit each day but why should there be a double standard? They say they are rewarding return customers but I say I'm not buying that excuse or anything else from them. I wish they would put themselves in our shoes and think about how tourists feel about paying higher prices than the locals for the same merchandise. This is how places get reputations, good and bad.

Many towns around the nation could take heed of this next thought. We all understand that competition makes prices drop and services improve. Having said that, it often seems to me that town councils and planning commissions have an obligation to the established businesses to help them thrive. Too much competition for the same dollar can mean that the individual businesses each get less. If your town has two convenience stores and they both seem to be doing well, should you then expect eight convenience stores all to thrive in the same place? How many fast food places can survive before we start to see boarded up buildings? In too many towns the local planning commissions are asleep at the wheel. I wish they would wake up and steer development.

Caledonia:

Caledonia is proof that my general statement above is not always true. This pretty little place is almost completely comprised of antique shops and, as such, it has become a destination. Pickers and shoppers will be attracted to a cluster of antique dealers. A good scenic highway lined with antiques is truly a "draw".

Have you heard people speak of the beauty of other states? Of course you have. Sometimes it's irritating because we know that our prairies, hills, and rivers are beautiful also but they don't get credit for that. If you have visited some other place by automobile and then returned to Missouri you may realize why we don't get that positive recognition.

My wife and I returned from a few weeks of driving through Ireland and were talking on the plane. As we spoke of the green hills of that place, I couldn't help but think of the green hills of home. Ours are higher and tree-covered. Our streams are just as fresh as theirs and we have more caves and lots more sunshine. As we drove from the airport and into the countryside, it became obvious to me that the major difference between Missouri and other places is the gaudy billboards that line our roads and block our view of nature's beauty. They even detract from the attractive and interesting structures created by man. Have you ever seen those plastic-draped monsters after a strong wind storm? I wish our state would begin a program to limit and eradicate most of the billboards.

Hermann:

Hermann and other communities as well as neighborhoods in the big cities and county fairs must stop thinking that they are doing something good for the community by providing venues for binge drinking. Festivals and fairs are ruined by obnoxious behavior, profanity, and vomit. I understand that some people make money but what about the loss of civility and the drunken drivers? What about the property damage? What about the families that unknowingly get exposed to indecent behavior? I wish that cities and towns were cracking down on public intoxication – not encouraging it.

This writer especially condemns the degradation of the St. Patrick's Day festivities. I have attended parades in Missouri cities for years and have enjoyed the family atmosphere as families and clans don their matching clothing and march, or create floats to celebrate their Celtic heritage. But the television stations covering the parades always focus on the most insane behavior and costumes for their interviews. They ignore the families who really make the event. Over the years the various St. Pat's events have come to be more and more about green beer and leprechauns and less and less about Irish heritage. We Irish-Americans resent the hijacking of our holiday by drunks.

St Louis and Missouri Counties:

The very worst is the day when family neighborhoods are taken over by drinking, public nudity, and public toileting in the name of Mardi Gras. **St. Louis** is the worst for this and city leaders seem to be impotent or un-caring when it comes to controlling drunken partiers. There is no reason for this situation to continue and I wish the leaders in St. Louis would give the order to let the police do their jobs,

Counties around the state need to exercise more control over junk yards. Call them what you like, it doesn't change the fact that these places are ugly. Salvage is an important part of a technological society but important and attractive are not the same thing. I remember Lady Bird Johnson insisting that junk yards be enclosed by a solid fence. Whatever happened to those laws and ordinances? Lady Bird, we need you again!

Now, back to the good stuff!

Labadie

Over 200 years ago a little settlement took shape at the Missouri River in present day Franklin County. Among the pioneers in this neighborhood were Dan, John and Joseph McCoy; Henry, Adam and Jacob Zumwalt (Fort Zumwalt); John Day; George Pursley; John Ridenhour and Peter Pritchett. The community was named for Sylvester L'Abbadie, reported to have died in a nearby cave while bear hunting. On April 3, 1803 the place was attacked by Indians and John Ridenhour was killed. The settlement was immediately abandoned but re-populated later in the Fall of that same year.

In 1804 Lewis and Clark were making their way upstream but were apparently not aware of the town. The explorers stopped across the river at Boone's Settlement and just downstream at Charrette Village. Maybe they by-passed Labadie because they thought it was still abandoned. Just upstream from Labadie (nearer present day St. Albans) Meriwether Lewis had the day before fallen from a 300 foot bluff at Tavern Cave then "caught himself by his knife" just 20 feet from certain death.

As two centuries passed, not much happened in Labadie except for the good everyday activities of farmers, merchants, ministers and others whose pride kept the little community in good shape and prosperous. Arriving in Labadie today is like arriving in a spot in history. The wood frame buildings contain some real surprises. Maybe the best is the Hawthorne Inn. While it can be a little pricey, the meals are a real treat! And it must be admitted that the menu's price range is very broad. A dish at the Hawthorne is a treat, no matter what the price level. The casual atmosphere and the outstanding menu are worth the trip from I-44.

There are other interesting businesses also. A popular tavern is always jumping, the old train station has shopping surprises and Labadie Station has classes and lots of Missouri-made crafts. The Tin Rabbit has outstanding antiques and furnishings. Good B&Bs and the neatest little grocery store you've seen in a while.

If you drive in Franklin, St. Charles, St. Louis, or Warren Counties you have seen the three gigantic smokestacks looming from somewhere in the countryside. Actually, you are seeing the Ameren UE electrical generating plant at Labadie. It provides power for St. Louis and much of east central Missouri

By far the biggest attraction at Labadie is Purina Farms (Gray Summit). This huge facility is a great place for a family field trip. You can get up close and personal with all kinds of farm animals and pets. Of course this is a research facility and there are lots of interesting on-going experiments and the guides are happy to answer your questions. This experience is free but you should call ahead to make reservations.

Individual Attractions

These attractions are singular places in or near small towns. While the town itself may not be suitable for a write-up in this book, these attractions may be worth a side trip if you happen to be in the area.

First things first. If you are a Missouri resident but have not taken the free tours of the **Capitol Building** and the **Governor's Mansion**, do that now. Let your Senator and representative know you're coming and you might get a moment with them to express your view on an important issue. Tour the free museum in the Capitol Building. At lunch time go over to the Truman Office Building and enjoy their cafeteria. If you are so inclined, take a tour of the old penitentiary just a few blocks away. I find it fascinating. Then, before you start home, cross over to the south side of the expressway and get a real ice cream treat at the Central Dairy.

Individual Attractions (cont.) Kingdom City's Fire Fighter's Memorial

You probably know the story of Callaway County in the War Between the States. This community was so un-divided in its loyalty to their cause that they told the opposing armies to stay away. They would police themselves and not enter into the fighting. They were armed to the teeth and spoke from a position of power. Outsiders began to refer to this rural county as the Kingdom of Calloway.

When a point of intersection was chosen for highways 40 and 54, it was at the little village of McCredie. When the highway was actually built, folks called the place "The Y." Then, with tax revenues available from the numerous cafes, gas stations, and dance halls, a fight was underway as some wanted the place to be incorporated as "North Fulton" and others lobbied for "South McCredie." Eventually they settled on the name of Kingdom City and McCredie's post office moved there.

Individual Attractions (cont,) Kingdom City's Fire Fighter's Memorial

Today there is an exit from I-70 right at the small (population 120) town called Kingdom City. Besides some very good truck stops, convenience stores, and souvenir shops, there is one of the best and cleanest tourist information centers to be found. It even has a small museum inside. To this writer the best thing in Kingdom City is the statue adjacent to the information center.

Fire Fighter's Memorial

Individual Attractions (cont.)
Kingdom City's Fire Fighter's Memorial

There, under the flags of Missouri and the US is a very large bronze statue of a fireman on one knee. Under the statue are listed the names of fallen fire fighters from throughout our state's history. It's very impressive and inspiring but there's even more to this statue's story.

You see, this is really a second casting of the original statue. The first was to be installed and dedicated in 2001. Then came the tragic events of September 11 that year. The first responders at that Manhattan tragedy were all in great peril and many of them lost their lives. In the nation's hurry to celebrate their bravery and recognize their losses, it was suggested that the original large statue be erected in New York rather than Kingdom City. It was done and now the identical statue graces the prairie land there in central Missouri. Why not stop for a minute and sign the guestbook?

Individual Attractions (cont.)
Fort Davidson

Literally across the road from Ironton is a strange looking donut-shaped mound of dirt known as Fort Davidson. This Civil War fort was hastily constructed in an ancient redoubt (earthen fortress) form so a few Union troops could make a stand against General Sterling Price's advancing Confederates. At stake was the capture of the unprepared St. Louis and Jefferson City.

A truly amazing story took place on that little spot below the knob of a hill. Called the Battle of Pilot Knob, it is a story worth knowing and an experience worth living to climb the redoubt and picture what happened on that site. It's all free and open to the family. The site is well-marked with historical facts and information.

While you're in the area, check out Ironton on the other side of the highway. It's a pretty historic place itself. Fortunes made from Iron mining and wealthy St. Louisans arriving by train have left the town with some unique architecture in the antebellum homes, churches, and even the battle-scarred courthouse.

Individual Attractions (cont.)
Meramec Caverns

I don't have much in this book about commercial enterprises but Meramec Caverns is a very special place and an important part of what Missouri actually has become. Known by many as "The Cave State," Missouri does have more than 7,000 caves and many of them are commercially developed. But this one has a unique history.

Of course the Osage knew of the place for thousands of years and many kinds of prehistoric animals inhabited the place but the first European-American to see it was a French miner in 1772. It had no real significance until the War Between the States when the Union Army was busy extracting saltpeter from the cave to be used in making gun powder. Confederate guerillas including a young Jesse James arrived and put a stop to that. It is thought that the James Brothers later returned and used the cave as a hideout.

Individual Attractions (cont.)
Meramec Caverns

A true showman, Lester Dill, bought the property in 1935 and began to promote it in memorable ways. He introduced what people called bumper stickers and hired people to arrange to paint farmers' barn roofs all across the nation for free. Of course these roofs advertised Dill's cave. Even today, there are more than fifty Meramec Caverns billboards along Interstate 44 alone! In 1960 the world's only underground billboards were rented out inside the caverns.

On March 10, 1950, Frank Dalton showed up in a Franklin County Courtroom claiming to be Jesse James. Rudy Turilli, (from Meramec Caverns) brought Dalton to live in a cabin at the cave. It was a good stunt but nothing more. This does, however, show the kind of creative advertising at work in this enterprise.

Having said all of this, let's remember a few things. First, this is an interesting and wonderful place. Second, the owners provide boat rides, zip lines, community days, and more to make your visit memorable. Third, everyone from Kate Smith to Lassie to the Beatles have been here. In fact more than 150,000 people each year take the tour. Probably you should too.

Individual Attractions (cont.)
White Squirrels

When the settlers first arrived in the seven springs area that we now call Marionville, they found unusual creatures. The place was full of albino squirrels! Today the squirrels lead a charmed life with huge oak trees, hundreds of newer nut trees, freshwater springs and local ordinances making it illegal to harm a squirrel.

In addition, local civic clubs furnish nesting boxes and feeders. The result is a town full of big white fluffy friendly squirrels. One town in Illinois claims to be the white squirrel something or other, but they have relatively few of the critters. You might go there and never see a white one. Another town in Tennessee makes a similar claim but its squirrels are much smaller.

The bottom line is this:

If you want to see lots of these cute little animals, just plan to spend a little time in Marionville!

Individual Attractions (cont.)
Stars and Stripes Museum

Bloomfield's historical claim to fame is the Battle of Bloomfield which was fought on November 7 and 8 of 1861. While the Illinois troops were looting the town one of them spotted a newspaper office with a printing press. They went in and set to work printing a newspaper for the Union soldiers. It was first distributed on Saturday morning, November 9 right there in Bloomfield and was the first edition of the famous *Stars and Stripes* newspaper which has served our armed forces ever since. "Read it and pass it to your buddy."

Today a nice modern museum sits right there on Highway 25 waiting for your visit.

Why not stop in?

<u>Individual Attractions (cont.)</u>
<u>Museum of the Unexplained</u>

If you're lucky you can catch this museum when it's in town. You see it moves from place to place. What else would you expect from a museum of mysterious things? Reed Springs is the original home of the place but it now has a bus and its full-time staff spends much of the year on the road.

In the museum you can see all sorts of information about crop circles, UFOs, etc. The main draw is an unexplained piece of metal alloy. Museum owners claim that it is not of this earth. They say it seems to have fallen from spacecraft.

How often do you get to see something like that?

Individual Attractions (cont.)
BoatHenge

You have probably pulled off the Interstate at Rolla and seen the Stone Henge there. It's interesting but not too impressive. It was a project of some folks at the Missouri University of Science and Technology and it gave them practice in cutting stone with high pressure water and abrasives. But it is not the only henge in our state.

On the Little Bonne Femme Creek near the Missouri River between Rocheport and Jefferson City there can be found a BoatHenge. Promoters explain that these six boats with their noses buried and their tails erect just appeared on the Spring Solstice by either springing up from the ground or dropping from the sky. They aren't sure and their story doesn't matter a whole lot, does it?

At any rate it's at least as interesting as lawn jockeys or pink flamingoes. BoatHenge is best viewed from the Katy Trail.

Individual Attractions (cont.)
Pumpkin Festival

Another small community on the Katy Trail, Hartsburg, (population 103) throws a big party each year and over 10,000 people usually show up for the fun. For a quarter of a century now, this pleasant little German community in Boone County has run a family-oriented group of wagon rides to the pumpkin patch and a street lined with booths featuring Missouri crafts, food, games, and music. Of course, a pumpkin festival would have to be in October but you will want to check their website for details.

<u>Individual Attractions (cont.)</u>
<u>Trumpeter Swans</u>

For years the Mississippi and Missouri rivers have been the winter home of the majestic bald eagles. They fish and nest along the bluffs and treetops for as long as the river is open and at least partially free of ice. Now they have company. At the juncture of the two largest rivers in North America the Trumpeter Swans have returned. These beautiful birds have a length of over five feet with better than a six and one-half foot wingspan. Their call sounds much like a French horn

To spend some time with the trumpeter swans and their bald eagle neighbors just go north through St. Louis County on Route 367 and take the very last turn (right) before crossing the river into Alton, IL. The bottom land there is state owned and is a wildlife refuge open to the public.

Individual Attractions (cont.)
The Ralph Foster Museum

On the campus of the College of the Ozarks in Point Lookout is the Ralph Foster Museum. It's a terrific museum with lots of things thought to be particularly interesting to Ozarkers. The best known exhibit is the actual 1921 Oldsmobile truck used in the original *Beverly Hillbillies* TV series. It was donated by the show's originator, Paul Henning, who grew up in Kansas City and, as a child, would often camp near here with his family.

If you go there, don't you dare miss the mill right on the campus. It's still operating and the students grind grain almost daily. You can also get an exceptional lunch at a very reasonable price on the campus. Of course you always have hamburger joints nearby. I know which one I would choose.

Individual Attractions (cont.)
Murals at Cuba

If you're traveling down I-44 and looking for a place to stretch your legs, Cuba is a good choice. They have taken very seriously the job of painting everything in town with murals depicting their history. Lots of towns do this now but not many do it well. This Route 66 town has done it very well. Cuba has interesting things to learn by looking at their artwork. It seems that every interesting thing in the area has been "muralized." The best way see the murals, is to stop by the visitor's center and ask for the brochure which has a map and description of the significance of each painting. You will be pleasantly surprised. If you stay on old Route 66 and go west for four miles you come to Fanning where you can find the four-story rocking chair described in the "Giants…" section.

Individual Attractions (cont.)
The Puxico Library.

On Highway 51 West of Throwed Rolls and East of Lake Wappapello there sits the little village of Puxico. This little town has an interesting and beautiful little city library. It opened in 1939 and is constructed of cypress logs chinked with white and painted red. Yes, it's air-conditioned and carpeted and has high-speed internet but it is truly a log building. The word "charming" really fits this place.

The Library at Puxico

Individual Attractions (cont.)
The Old Stage Stop

As people patiently scour the roadsides for glimpses of anything reminding them of Route 66, they often pass right by something that predates Route 66 by many decades. Back before there was a Route 66 the road was called the Wire Road. Prior to that it was called the Military Road and in those days stage coaches made their way through the Ozarks with stops at places like Jerome, Antioch, and Waynesville.

Waynesville had the best place for travelers. Its stage stop was a big two-story inn with a restaurant and it was right on the courthouse square so other amenities were available also. Since those days it has become a hospital for Civil War soldiers, a barracks for construction workers building Fort Leonard Wood and much more. And it's still there for you to see and tour. A group of local residents and many schoolchildren have worked to preserve it all for you. When you go, ask about the town square hangings.

Individual Attractions (cont.)
Caveman Barbeque

If you dig it, they will come. Not far from the Old Stage Stop there is a pretty good restaurant actually located in a cave! Near Richland, **The Cave Restaurant** sits one hundred feet above the Gasconade River on Rochester Road. This restaurant features catfish, steaks, and some good barbeque. It actually seats 225 so if you're in the Lebanon-Fort Wood area, this would be a good place for a business luncheon. Oh yes, there is an elevator to take you up to the cave.

NOTE: As this second edition of *Too Good to Pass By* is being prepared, this special restaurant is closed for remodeling and maintenance work on the elevator. You might want to make a call, check on line, or ask one of the locals before making the trip.

Individual Attractions (cont.)
The Grand Falls

Missouri's largest waterfall is on the edge of Joplin. Grand falls only drops for twelve feet but it is over a hundred and sixty feet across. It is also a good one because it drops in two steps. In 1860 Shoal Creek was dammed up to create a huge mill pond for mills and later for hydro-electric power production. Today it is the city's water reservoir and a very popular place for floating, fishing, and other recreation. This is a pretty one so when you visit, bring your camera,

Old Mines

. My very first acquaintance with anything about Old Mines, Missouri was in my undergraduate days at Mizzou. In the administration building (Jesse Hall) there hangs a small painting of the general store at Old Mines. It reminded me of many of the little community stores at home which had seen better days but were still trying to be relevant in the days of dependable automobiles.

That old store is still there on Highways 21 and 47 but it's just a dry, rusty, vine-covered ghost of its former self. I'll bet that if walls could talk, it could tell some wonderful stories about this very old neighborhood.

In 1719 Sieur de Renaudiere conducted mining operations in the vicinity of the Meramec Valley, Big River and Washington County. He was sent here by the Company of the Indies but, lacking skilled workers, his mining operations were unsuccessful. In that same year Philip Francois Renault left France for Upper Louisiana (now called Missouri) bringing supplies and skilled miners. He stopped in the Caribbean and purchased slaves to work in the mines. These were the first slaves to be brought to Missouri.

The date of 1719 is also significant because it is sixteen years before the founding of Ste. Genevieve. Because of this, the people at Old Mines claim to be the oldest town in Missouri.

The real heart of Old Mines is the St. Joachim Church. This imposing brick building was built in 1830 and is still the spiritual home for about 350 families. The main reason for visiting Old Mines is found immediately behind the church. Here, well-preserved cabins and log buildings can be seen and identifying signs are written in French so there can be no question about how this community came to be.

Between some of the cabins are actual working beehive ovens for baking bread and other things. To see them in operation, you need to contact the church or look up the festival days for Old Mines. Even if you don't see them working, it's a treat just to see them at all!

Creole French was still spoken here until the 1940s and the colloquial blue and white garb was worn. That is all history now but these folks are helping us to remember a time gone by.

Lexington

Don't drive through this town. Drive throughout this town. It is full of treats for your eyes. Better yet, get out and spend some time. It's full of unique places and the sites of historic events. After all, it was at one time the largest town west of St. Louis.

In 1819 William Jack operated a ferry boat and the new town of Lexington was platted in 1822 at the dock for that ferry. Hemp, tobacco, cotton, and cattle were the earliest agricultural pursuits here. These products reflected the Kentucky roots of the first citizens. Sadly, this also meant the arrival of slaves and, if you look closely, you will still see the little slave cottages behind some of Lexington's older homes.

Be careful now, not to mistake the summer kitchens for slave quarters. Summer kitchens were used by the wise folks in Missouri's hot summers. They were a place for food to be cooked without heating up the entire house. Today I suppose the barbeque grill has taken over some of those duties.

During the years from 1830 to 1850 Lexington was the major supplier to people traveling westward on the California Trail, the Oregon Trail, the Santa Fe Trail, and the Mormon Trail. In the 1850s the largest trading firm in the west was headquartered on Main Street. The partners in this firm, Russell, Majors, and Waddell, had more than 3500 wagons, more than 4000 employees, over 40,000 oxen and more than 10,000 mules. They were known as "The Mariners of the Plains." These three men also went on to establish the Pony Express from St. Joe to Sacramento. You can read more about them in my book, *Tales From Missouri and the Heartland*.

Steamboating was not possible on the Missouri River until people learned how to design and build a special variety of boats. From then on, river traffic increased and Lexington's riverfront dock became a center of commerce. In 1852 the Missouri River's worst disaster took place at Lexington. The steamboat Saluda was carrying 250 Mormons toward Salt Lake City when its boilers exploded killing over 150. Many children were orphaned that day and were adopted into the families of Lexington.

The Battle of the Hemp Bales took place at Lexington during the War Between the States. Creative Confederates under the command of Sterling Price wetted bales of hemp and rolled them toward the Union military forces creating moving breastworks. The strategy worked and Price's forces won the day. A cannon ball from that battle still can be seen high on one of the Courthouse Pillars and has come to be the symbol of the town. The Second Battle of Lexington was fought there three years later.

Of course the Civil War must bring the mention of Quantrill's Raiders, Jesse and Frank James, Cole Younger, and Archie Clement, all of whom were frequent "visitors" to Lexington. The war and the period of turmoil that followed hampered Lexington's growth but the beautiful homes and other buildings from that day can be seen all over the town.

Also adding to Lexington's architectural heritage was its position as the "Athens of the West." So called because of its four colleges, it attracted many upper class citizens but not enough students. Today only one of the colleges remains. Wentworth Military Academy is still home to many fine young men from all over the world.

So, why visit Lexington today? Because today you can stroll down the very streets where wagon trains once rolled and shop in buildings dating back to the 1840s. Many of these buildings are listed on the National Register of Historic Places. You can see antebellum homes that look like something from a movie. To this writer Lexington is a special place with a unique character coming from its river, its architecture, and its very colorful history.

GONE: But Not Forgotten

This may seem to be a strange chapter for a book such as this. The items which follow are all things which you can no longer see in Missouri. I include them to make a point – We should endeavor to see things and have experiences now because many things are fleeting. If you want to have lunch on the **McDonalds Riverboat** Restaurant, you've missed the boat. It's long gone. Some places are truly worth remembering so get out there and make those memories now!

The **Kohler City Store** near Barnhart was a one-of-a-kind kind of place. It was an old-fashioned store right on the main north & south highway between St. Louis and Cape Girardeau. Among the other interesting things there were two barrels. One contained used eye glasses which were available for sale. The other barrel contained used false teeth that people could try on and put back until they found a pair that fit. Take a minute and think about that one! I was told but don't remember artificial legs hanging there for sale also. Who says the old-timers didn't recycle valuable commodities?

The **Oakland Store** in Laclede County was a wooden two-story building where a boy could find things like Grapette, Orange Crush, and Dreamsicles. I'll bet you know of a neat little country store that used to be. If you still know of a good one, take your kids or grand-kids there today and often. A personal favorite today is the old company store at St. Albans.

GONE: BUT NOT FORGOTTEN

(CONT.)

Garber, Missouri was a little community roughly between present day Branson and Silver Dollar City. It is claimed by some to have been the origin of the Silver Dollar City development. While Harold Bell Wright was a minister at Lebanon and at Pierce City he often visited the folks at Garber. He used these people and this place as the basis for his book, *The Shepherd of the Hills.*

You may have seen the performances of this story or read one of the millions of books sold telling this tale. More likely you have seen one of the five motion pictures made depicting the story. One happened to be Gary Cooper's first major film. The best was probably the one starring John Wayne. It also featured Marjorie Main, Ward Bond, and Fuzzy Knight. The problem with that one, however, is that the characters are not at all like the characters in the novel. But it's still a good story.

Old Matt, Young Matt, Sammy Lane and all of the others lived and visited in this characteristic Ozark community. The little town's band is pictured on the next page.

GONE: BUT NOT FORGOTTEN

(CONT.)

Photo courtesy of "Preserve Our Past Society," El Dorado Springs1

This traditional band has no trumpets but five cornets on the second row. The first row shows two drums and three clarinets. The back row has a tuba, two baritone horns, a double-belled euphonium (Yes, it has two bells!), French horn, two alto horns, a valve trombone (no slide) and an old instrument called a helicon. The helicon was a military-style tuba that could be played on horseback.

Ash Grove

Way back in 1853 Kimbrough's Store opened on Main Street in Ash Grove but that and a blacksmith shop were about all there was as far as business there until after the War Between the States. Read more about this interesting town just northwest of Springfield.

As early as 1837 the Ash Grove area was getting notable new residents. Most notable among them was Nathan Boone, the youngest son of Daniel Boone. Nathan actually built a dogtrot cabin here in 1837 and he and Daniel often came to hunt until Daniel's age was prohibitive. Nathan and his wife, Olive, lived here for most of their adult lives and are buried on the farm. Today you can visit their graves and walk through the comfortable cabin built by Nathan, Daniel, and some of their slaves. As a State Historic Site, it's open and free to the public.

The Ozarks Afro-American Museum is another Ash Grove place to visit. The very personable Father Moses Berry founded the museum and will likely be your guide. Genetic tests show that he is a direct descendent of one of the Boone men and one of the slaves. The museum has always been right on Main Street in Ash Grove but it struggles financially and has moved into temporary quarters. Ask someone locally about the exhibits and visit. This little museum is unique and worth the stop.

Following the War in 1865 Settlement increased in the area. One reason was the abundance of jobs at the nearby Phenix Quarry. The ghost town of Phenix, Missouri is located in Greene County, close to Ash Grove. Phenix was a company town that existed for the sole purpose of mining marble and limestone from the adjacent quarry. It was unique in that the town had a library, an orchestra, movies, and a church with a full-time minister. Bonnie Parker of Bonnie and Clyde fame was a resident of Phenix and even attended elementary school there for a time.

Today, the quarry is still in use for crushed stone and a few of the old buildings still remain, but the town itself has ceased to exist. Of particular interest at this site are the original lime kilns and the remains of a once-thriving company town (with a population of approximately 500) that disappeared during the Great Depression.

Marble from this historic quarry was used to build the Missouri State Capitol, the New York Stock Exchange, San Francisco's Russ Building, the Petroleum Securities building in

Los Angeles, Kansas City's Southwestern Bell Telephone Building, and other well-known buildings across the United States.

The Ash Grove Cement Company started in 1882 in Ash Grove, Missouri, under the name Ash Grove White Lime Association. Today Ash Grove is the largest American-owned producer of cement and the sixth largest producer of cement in the United States but it's no longer in Ash Grove.

The post war growth in Ash Grove was spurred by the arrival of the Kansas City/Clinton/Springfield Railroad. Its main function was to haul the high quality stone from the quarry but it also carried some passengers. Known locally as the "Leaky Roof Railroad," it must not have been tuned in to the comfort of the passengers.

A structural wonder is located four miles east of Ash Grove on Highway 160. Francis and Kannon Gilmore built the octagonal barn (also called "the round barn") between 1898 and 1907. The two-story building with wood and masonry construction is still functional, attractive, and interesting.

When the good citizens of Ash Grove finished with the octagonal barn, they turned to the building of a secure jail. You see, the original jail would not hold the prisoners. If not for that, what good is a jail? This time they built the jail with thick concrete walls which were reinforced with railroad springs.

The roof was constructed with railroad rails. No one ever escaped from this building. This jail known as "The Cooler" is there for you to see if you want. It's not pretty but it was very functional.

Now I mentioned earlier that Bonnie Parker lived nearby. She wasn't the only notorious woman for sure! The queen bee of a pack of mongrels, Arizona Clark, was born in Ash Grove. Known locally as Arrie, she became known everywhere else as "Ma Barker." Though probably not the mastermind of the Ma Barker Gang, she was an accomplice and helped them travel and do their dirty work without getting caught.

So the next time you're near Springfield, swing over to this little town which has been home to notorious women, famous pioneers, and one of the best limestone/marble quarries anywhere.

Dining with History in St.Louis

. There are many good excuses for dining in St. Louis and this one seems as good as any. St. Louis has been the site of the creation and/or introduction of many foods. In this writer's view, we can thank the eclectic mix of cultures that came together in the Mound City and their willingness to enjoy "what's cooking" in the neighbor's kitchen. Add to that the fact that the city has always been a crossroads and a gateway for travelers using every possible mode of transportation.

As I propose these dining suggestions, watch for the ethnic influence, as well as the ways that transportation has influenced where the foods became popular and how they spread. From the river roads, to the railroads, to the Mother Road, and beyond, Africans, Chinese, French, Germans, Irish, and of course the Italians have made their contributions to the Historian's Day of Dining.

In my dream days of eating the signature foods which originated in St. Louis, I would start with a slinger. This he-man breakfast (also great as a lunch, dinner, or snack) combines eggs, hash browns, and then a hamburger patty. All of this is topped with chili, cheese, and some chopped onions. It's been copied and called a skillet breakfast or in a different form, it might be a western omelet but the St. Louis slinger set the pace right here back in 1935 at the Courtesy Sandwich Shop.

Instead of Sandwich Shops, the three locations are now called Courtesy Diners. This writer's personal favorite is at 1121 Hampton Avenue, just a stone's throw south of the St. Louis Zoo. This location has that '50s diner feel with stools, a juke box and everything else you would expect. The diner at 3155 South Kingshighway is a little older and clearly shows its Route 66 tradition. It is also easier to find a spot to park your car. The third location is at the intersection of Watson and Laclede Station Roads and it's a jewel too.

Since the Slinger was created, Courtesy has grown, modified its name, and added to its menu. So now you can get the original Slinger or one of three other varieties. The Hoosier Slinger is served with white gravy instead of chili and therefore, a breakfast favorite for some. The Hangover Slinger is a late night favorite and it resembles the Hoosier with the addition of a chicken fried steak patty. Finally there is the Devil's Delight which has no hamburger or steak but is still topped with that good Edmond's Chili.

At this point you are right between the Zoo, the Dogtown Neighborhood with its Irish roots, the upscale Central West End, and the Italian Hill. All are good places to walk off that big breakfast and to reconnect with much of the city's history. You will also want to be aware that the Zoo is in Forest Park which contains the free Missouri Historical Society Museum and the free St. Louis Art Museum.

For lunch, let's pay a visit to the Lafayette Square neighborhood. Actually just a few blocks north of there at Chouteau and 14th street is a terrific little place. Many years ago Steven Yuen at Park Chop Suey concocted something that he named the St. Paul Sandwich. Now, don't be afraid to go in this place. It's not the place to impress your date but you and your buddies will love the food so it's worth it. There are no tables but there is one "L" shaped counter about four feet high so you can stand there, if you like, to enjoy your steaming hot food.

Of course you will want to pay attention to the hand-written signs instructing you not to sit on that counter, or not to use your cell phone, or not to use the restroom. But the signs include the misspelled word "Plesae" just to be polite. But enough of that. Let's talk about the food. You will want to get a St. Paul Sandwich for sure and you can choose what kind of meat that you prefer. I highly recommend the pork. In a paper bag, wrapped in clean white paper you will receive two slices of white bread with an egg foo yung omelet patty, lettuce, tomato, dill pickle slice, white onion, and mayonnaise on the side. It's a hot, slightly crunchy, and wonderful tasty treat! Get three of their famous triangle Crab Rangoon and you'll thank yourself for the rest of the day.

I mentioned that you could stand at the counter and eat but why not take your lunch and find a shady spot over at Lafayette park? This beautiful old park surrounded by beautiful townhouses is the place where some gentlemen played the very first game of baseball west of the Mississippi. If your timing is good you can even watch the St. Louis Perfectos play one of their rivals from the Greater St. Louis Base Ball Historical Society. If you're really lucky, you'll see them play the St. Louis Brown Stockings or the St. Louis Unions. Rules from the 1860s are used and it's easy to tell that it was a game for gentlemen back in the day.

After a day of walking and baseball you'll be ready for dinner at any Imo's Pizza. This is the home of the St. Louis style pizza which is different from pizza anywhere else.

For one thing, the hot pizza is cut into squares and never wedges. St. Louis pizza is all about the ingredients and not about the crust. The crust on a St. Louis pizza is thin and it has only one main purpose – it an edible platform to hold all the good stuff. Chief among the "good stuff" ingredients would be

Provel cheese. This is a St. Louis invention and is sold almost nowhere else in the nation.

Provel was invented specifically for use on pizza. It was designed back in the 1940s by Ed Imo's uncle, John Sigillito, to have "a clean bite" and to compliment the other flavors on the pie. After much experimentation he decided on just the proper blend of cheddar, Swiss, and Provolone. John ran the Costa Grocery (now Roma's Grocery) and was the sole distributor for many years. Now Kraft Foods owns the brand. Sigillito made up the name "Provel" and no one knows why he chose that but there have been many guesses over the years. In fact, his original patent was denied because the name of the product had no meaning.

When we've had our fill, we'll get a "To Go" box and take the rest of the pizza with us as we explore the historic Hill neighborhood. Originally this little place was a communist community established by a Frenchman, Etenne Cabet, and his followers who called themselves Icarians. When that experiment failed, the immigrant Irish took the northern part of the area which we now call Dogtown. Italians took the southern part of the area. That's why the colors of the Italian flag are everywhere.

You will want to visit Hall of Fame Street (a.k.a. the west end of Elizabeth Street) whose tidy little houses were the homes of young Jack Buck, Joe Garagiola, and Yogi Berra. Those names are still prominent in St. Louis. "The Immigrants" is a famous statue in front of St. Ambrose church in this neighborhood and the St. Elizabeth's Church is also a pillar of the community. I can never go to the Hill without picking up some pastries at the Missouri Baking Company and the fresh meats at Volpi Salami Store. In my mind, the best of the best.

Of course no historian or food lover would leave the Hill without at least a snack of toasted ravioli. You can get good versions of this at any of the Italian restaurants in St. Louis but we want to visit the home of the St. Louis treat. Some will say that Charlie Gitto's is the birthplace but this writer thinks another spot is more likely and this place features St. Louis' most famous waiter.

Joe Garagiola's big brother, Mickey, was the announcer for decades on the "Wrestling at the Chase" TV program. His day job was as a waiter. In the 1940s he was working at Oldani's (Now "Mamma's on the Hill" at Edwards and Bischoff) when a chef, Terry Lane, messed up a ravioli order. He is said to have knocked the pasta into a deep fryer instead of putting them in to boil. Mickey tasted them anyway and declared that, with some seasoning, they would be a hit. Toasted ravioli was born as a St. Louis tradition. So let's have a snack of the toasted (really deep fried) treat and then, since beer is such an important part of the local history, give in and enjoy any of the local brews while we're at it.

For the rest of the day, a person would have to make a painful decision as to how his or her time could best be spent. St. Louis is home to more free attractions than any other city except for Washington, D.C. If a person with an inerest in history has already visited the St. Louis Riverfront and Laclede's Landing, then I would consider the very historic Jefferson Barracks. For the place with the most appeal, I suppose I would recommend going a little to the west and taking the long walk through the Museum of Transportation.

For a second day of dining with history, just chose your favorite breakfast or try one of the brunches that St. Louisans love. Whenever you're ready for lunch, let's head for what became famous as the Mayfair Hotel. The elegant place has been renamed as the Magnolia Hotel by its new owners. It has been the home-away-from-home for Presidents, movie stars, and business people for decades. It was here that Cary Grant tried to seduce a local woman by leaving a trail of chocolates which ended up on his pillow. This is how we got the American tradition of chocolates on hotel pillows.

I must mention another historic fact about this place. When KMOX Radio used the Mayfair for its studios, they did something new and special. They invited two guests, the Mayor and Margaret Truman. Then they invited the listeners to call in and ask questions of the guests. Talk radio was born!

But let's get back to dining. Here you can choose from the famous Mayfair Salad or the Prosperity Sandwich. Both were invented right here by Mayfair chefs. The salad is fairly small but the sandwich is very filing. If you're with someone, you might want to split the two and share. Truth be told, the Mayfair Salad is served all over America and the Prosperity Sandwich is served at any good Italian restaurant but this is where they were born.

The Prosperity Sandwich is a little bit of a slam for the F.D.R. Administration who kept promising that prosperity was just around the corner and that happy days were here again. So the hotel chef created an open face turkey, ham, and bacon sandwich with melted cheese and a cream sauce. Some places leave off the sauce and that's too bad.

Now that Famous-Barr is just a memory, a few places continue to make the wonderful Famous-Barr French Onion Soup. This is a great place to get that also.

St. Louie Gooey is a real treat and the truth is that gooey butter cake is found in many places and, even thought it was created by a mistake, no one now seems able to make a bad version. The Magnolia and probably a hundred other places now serve the St. Louis original. Paula Dean gets a degree of fame for her "Original" Gooey Butter Cake but, even she, grudgingly admits that her first gooey butter cakes were from St. Louis and that's where she got her recipe.

There are two stories of the creation of the dessert and both of them center around South St. Louis during the Great Depression. The most likely account is that the German baker, John Hoffman, instructed a new employee to follow the recipe and make some coffee cakes called deep butter cakes. The new worker accidentally poured in a glue-like "gooey butter" adhesive coating that was used to make sprinkles and other decorations stick.

Being unwilling to throw out the expensive ingredients, Hoffman decided to bake the mixture and find out what it produced. He marketed the concoctions as gooey butter bars and they were an instant success. Soon every bakery in the city was producing them.

After visiting a few of the city's best attractions, it's time for dinner. Let's go for some St. Louis Barbeque. Missouri has three styles of barbeque and it's enjoyable to debate the merits of each. You might be familiar with the other styles. In the Ozarks many people serve a smoked meat, often pulled, on a bun. There might be no sauce at all but the sandwich is topped with cole slaw.

In western Missouri they have the Kansas City style with its thick, dark, and sweet molasses sauce. But, after all we're in St. Louis today where it all about the smoke and then a generous crowning of a red, vinegar-laced sauce.

Even more important in the St. Louis style is what meat you use. The traditional favorite here is pork steaks. That is a special cut of pork shoulder that cooks up to be very tender. When visiting in places like L.A. or New York, you are bound to see restaurants specializing in St. Louis-style barbeque and the one thing those places have in common is pork steaks. That cut of meat just isn't available in most cities.

The spare ribs found in St. Louis are also somewhat unique. They are cut so that each portion is a rectangular "slab" that's attractive and delicious. If you can get some barbeque and a side of baked beans made with "burnt ends" you may be ruined for all other food. Basic and wonderfully flavorful! Historically African-Americas and Italians have some pretty strong claims on the origins of St. Louis-style barbeque. But I prefer to believe that the meat wouldn't be as good if not for the influence of both traditions.

Well, that's certainly enough food for this trip. But wait! We haven't had a Ted Drewes concrete, or a brain sandwich, No Bissinger's Chocolates. You see, there's just no way to get through even the best of the St. Louis historic originals in just one trip. And, even in two or three trips, we would probably end up needing some Tums – another St. Louis original.

Wyota (Lebanon)

Most of the towns in this book are little-known places, "off the beaten path." This town however, is right on Interstate 44 and at the junction of Highway 5, Highway 32, and highway 64. It addition to that, it used to be a main stop on Route 66. But hundreds of years ago it was also located on an important road which was literally a "beaten path."

When this town was an Indian village named Wyota, it was part of an Osage trail that ran from the mounds where St. Louis now stands to the Ozarks Plateau near where Springfield is today. Wyota Village was at the edge of a large sinkhole which can still be seen in the Old Town section. This sinkhole was thought to be one eye of the Great Spirit and the other eye, Bennett Spring, cried because of our behavior. Most of the businesses moved and newer homes were built to the south when the Frisco Railroad arrived.

The white man later made the Osage Trail into a road. Since the work was done by the military, it was called the Military Road. Then a telegraph wire was strung from tree to tree along the roadside and locals, proud of their high-tech place in the world, began to call it the Wire Road. Even today transportation is an important part of the place with its highways, a railroad, a jet port and five companies manufacturing boats. It's also the birthplace of the cowboy's favorite, Lee Wranglers blue jeans.

In addition to transportation, another significant element in this town's history has been its preachers. One popular Baptist asked to have the town's name changed from Wyota to Lebanon, thus honoring his former hometown in Tennessee. Another early Lebanon minister was Lemuel Sutton Reed, a Methodist, whose little son Walter Reed lived here then went on to become famous as a military surgeon and medical researcher.

The minister at the Christian Church (D.O.C.) in Lebanon was Harold Bell Wright who wrote many novels including Shepherd of the Hills which is performed daily at Branson At least twenty movies and one made-for-TV movie were made from Wright's stories. The best was probably the Shepherd of the Hills version which starred a young John Wayne.

The Baptist family of Rev. Dallas Vernon and his four sons (all ministers) did a syndicated television show called Homestead USA back in the early days of TV. Another unrelated Vernon minister, William Tecumseh Vernon, was a College president and Bishop of the A.M.E. Church in South Africa and the Midwest.

Erskine Caldwell was not from Lebanon but he wrote about time he spent there in his book, Afternoons in Mid-America. His unflattering portrayal dwelled on the importance of churches and ministers in the community. In that way, he was right on target. He claimed though that one local businessman told him that in Lebanon's early days there were only two good ways to make a living. One was farming but that was too much work. The other was preaching and that seemed to be the easy way to get money from all the farmers. I mention this only in humor because this writer grew up in Lebanon and the town's churches are an invaluable resource to the youth and adults alike.

Another famous resident of Lebanon was David Rice Malone who came to Laclede County as a child in about 1869. The old *Grit Magazine* dubbed him "the Corn King of the World." He was photographed climbing a sixteen-foot extension ladder to pick the ears off his corn. Some of the corn stalks were photographed in front of his post office and were taller than that building. With his corn he won first place at the State Fairs in Missouri, Illinois, and Iowa. Some of his corn was fed to his hogs which also brought home Grand Champion ribbons from State Fairs. His death brought letters of condolence from the Governors of three Midwestern states.

Richard Parks Bland was a famous Lebanon politician who lost his bid for US President in the last minute of his national convention. He is the namesake of many schools, streets and even of Bland, Missouri. More recently Phil M. Donnelley and Gene Paul Bradshaw both ran for Governor of Missouri. These two nominees of their respective parties had law offices directly across from each other on Madison Street. After the votes were counted it was seen that Donnelley got 1,731 votes in his home town. Bradshaw got exactly 1,731 also. But Donnelly got more statewide and eventually served two terms as the state's Chief Executive.

Lebanon has given many to the entertainment world also. Early groups like the Ozark Troubadours flourished here on the radio as well as better-known people like Larry Hooper in the age of television. Hooper was the piano-playing bass singer on the Lawrence Welk Program. The famous playwright, Lanford Wilson, was also born in Lebanon. Jazz bassist, Jim Widner, has played with some of the best bands in the world and is, at this writing, head of the Music Department at the University of Missouri – St. Louis. Syndicated radio talk show Hall of Famer, Jim Bohannon is also from Lebanon. He lives in the Washington, D.C. area now but is still active in

Lebanon's charity and social endeavors. Did you know that he is a darned good trombone player?

Ozark Airlines founder and philanthropist, Floyd Jones, and Ernest R. Breech, of the Ford Motor Company and the founder of the Breech School of Business at Drury University are Lebanon success stories. John Boswell tapped into a demand for oak, hickory, and walnut barrels needed in the winemaking and distilleries of Missouri and the surrounding states. His barrel stave plant and famous walnut bowls side product have pulled thousands of tourists off the road for a visit. John F. O'Reilly of the O'Reilly Automotive chain was also a Lebanon resident. All of these men have been generous with their donations to schools and universities in Lebanon and Springfield.

Having said all of this, I still have not mentioned the things which bring most people to Lebanon today. The nearby Lake of the Ozarks and Bennett Spring draw people to the natural beauty of the Ozarks Plateau. In the days of Route 66 there were signs at both ends of the town reading, "Lebanon, Our Town – Your Town." To this day, once you get past the fast food places, you will find some very friendly people who appreciate your visit.

Williamsburg

Willamsburg is the perfect illustration of the theme of this book. It's only one-half mile from Interstate 70 where tens of thousands of people zip past daily and too few stop to enjoy what they can find in this very interesting little hamlet. At exit 161 (just east of Kingdom City) a person can turn north and less than a minute later be confronted with a place where you may want to spend an entire day. I'm speaking of Crane's Country Store.

Maybe you haven't yet been to Crane's Country Store in Williamsburg but that's understandable. They have been in business since 1899 but they moved a few years ago. That was 1926. They advertise "Boots, Bullets, Britches, and Bologna" and that's catchy but it doesn't begin to size them up. They sell all kinds of things including a little food but don't expect anything too fancy at Crane's. Their most famous entrée is the "1meat, 1 cheese, 2 dollar sandwich." If you try this sandwich, you will be delighted with the freshness of the great variety of meats and cheeses and with their quantity too. It's $2.00 well spent.

Browsing through this dusty heaven is such a treat that you will probably not want to go alone. This is an experience to be shared with someone. I swear that some of the things in that store must have been there since they opened in the century before last! You might want to pick up a new shirt or some shoe polish while you're there. If they don't have it, you probably don't really need it anyway. This place is a trip back to the spirit of a pioneer's general store. I'm compelled to add that the staff is extremely courteous and welcoming.

While you're there you simply must walk past the old millstones (from the 1800s) and visit the museum next door. It is housed in a building with a throwback café where you might expect Beaver Cleaver to walk in at any time but you're more likely to meet the local farmers congregating for coffee. The food is excellent but the dining area is surrounded by museum rooms. Did I say that they are all free?! It's probably time that you visited Crane's and made your own discoveries.

The big road in front of Crane's Country Store is called Highway D today but in the past it was the US Highway 40. Then, just one block north, is a street ingloriously called Road 184. Here you will find at least one building from the 1830s and the Gray Ghost Bed & Breakfast. The important thing about this street is that almost 200 years ago this was the Booneslick Trail. Old Dan'l and his sons produced salt at the Booneslick and transported it back for sale in St. Charles and

St. Louis. While taking a load east was done by boat, this was the route that everyone used in going west. It's mind-boggling to imagine all of the great pioneers who frequented that old trail.

More Individual Attractions
Frankenstein!

Frankenstein, Missouri has a great little hometown school and a gorgeous Catholic Church. What else? A big Halloween party. What else? Pretty scenery in the spring and fall and prosperous farms all around. So why go to Frankenstein? Because it's the only town with that name anywhere!

Named by an early settler, Gottfreid Franken, it's located north of Highway 100 and between Jefferson City and Hermann. If you've driven the north side of the river on Highway 94 then why not drive the south side and swing through Frankenstein just to say you've been there. Who do you know who can make that claim?

Individual Attractions (cont.)
River's Edge

OK. Here's another reason to visit Frankenstein. If you go a little east on Highway 100 you can then turn south on Route N or Route J. Where these two meet is a terrific little restaurant on the Gasconade River. It's called River's Edge and the name is accurate. One highlight of your visit is that as you arrive or leave you will need to cross the Gasconade on a tiny ferryboat. It's fun but the ferry is not dependable so check ahead.

NOTE: As this second edition of *Too Good to Pass By* is being prepared, the ferry boat mentioned just above is not in service. And sadly, this writer does not believe that the ferry will be put into operation again. Wouldn't you like to live near this pleasant little community and run a ferry for all the cheerful passengers?

So at River's Edge sip some cold ones while you wait for your meal (always very good) and visit with some casual, relaxed, and pleasant folks who routinely arrive from Jefferson City, Hermann, Washington, and the surrounding areas. Leave your cell phone in the car and enjoy this little haven on the river. B.T.W., with your meal, order a little individual loaf of bread. You'll be surprised and glad you did.

Individual Attractions (cont.)
Lost Valley Hatchery

This writer grew up near a state park fish hatchery and thought that it was huge. The Lost Valley Hatchery at Warsaw is in a completely different league! It has 971 acres of land and over 78 acres of water. It is one of the ten largest hatcheries in the nation and produces 15 million fish annually. The visitor's center has a 12,700 gallon aquarium and much more.

Here's something special for parents and grandparents. At this place you not only don't pay for admission, they even have freebies. They offer classes on all aspects of fishing including how to measure your record catch. Even the fishing and the equipment and the bait are provided free.

The Hatchery and Visitors Center is located just east of Highway 65 at the Truman Dam Access Road, on County Road 620, northeast of Warsaw.

Individual Attractions (cont.)
Sandy Creek Bridge

One of the few remaining covered bridges in the state is just west of Pevely and east of Highway 21. It's in Goldman, MO which is basically a ghost town. Maybe the easiest way to get there is to just get on Lemay Ferry Road and follow it almost to the end. It's a nice drive and the end of the road is rewarding. The beautiful old red bridge is on 205 acres of land with picnic tables. If you have trouble finding it, call (636) 464-2976. As a taxpayer, you own it so it's free. Why not have a picnic? Grandkids love to wade in the clear fresh stream and climb on the boulders at the water's edge.

Individual Attractions (cont.)
Big Oak Tree State Park

In 2011 the Corps of Engineers blew the levees open and flooded this area with sixteen feet of water! This was not as devastating as you might think because the vegetation here is naturally occurring in areas prone to floods. Now you can return to the steel grating walkways and walk among the towering hickory and oak trees.

Several trees in this park have the status of being champions because of their size. Though we hear about the oaks and hickories, this place has a persimmon tree which is 132 feet tall. The average persimmon is 60 feet tall. By the way, a good look at the state's list of champion trees shows that most of our largest trees are not in state parks at all. Most of them are in people's lawns or in cemeteries. So as you drive around the state, be sure to look for and appreciate these friendly giants.

Individual Attractions (cont.)
Towosahgy State Historic Site

Just a stone's throw from Big Oak Tree is this park near East Prairie that is home to ancient Indian mounds of the Mississippian Culture. Towosahgy is an Indian word that means "old town." The residents here lived off their farm crops, wild game, fish, persimmons, wild plums and a variety of nuts. That makes sense when you think of what this place offered to its inhabitants.

Individual Attractions (cont.)
Old Drum Statue

In a town with a big university, an impressive list of famous residents, and a long history, it's a dog that is most often associated with this place. You see, there was a resident who had trouble getting along with people. Then, when he argued with his brother-in-law, he decided to shoot the brother-in-law's valuable hunting dog and companion. This dog was named Old Drum.

The dog's owner sued for damages and an amazing trial transpired. On September 23, 1870, Warrensburg trial lawyer and Senator, George Vest, delivered his closing argument in the case. The statement became famous as the "Eulogy on a Dog." The heart-stirring argument won the case. Lawyers in this case included David Nation, (husband of Carrie Nation) Tom Crittenden, (later Missouri's Governor) and Francis Cockrell. (later at U.S. Senator) Also appearing at the trial was John Phillips. (later a U.S. Congressman) It was in this trial that the saying was born, "A man's best friend is his dog.

Today visitors to Warrensburg will want to stop at the courthouse lawn and see the statue of the original "man's best friend: "Old Drum".

Individual Attractions (cont.)
The Gypsy King's Grave

On Highway 72, just inside Rolla's City Cemetery, There is a grave whose tombstone says "Broadway." This is said to be the resting place of a Gypsy King who died while passing through town on Route 66. At times the grave is highly decorated with bright flowers, carved wooden birds, and other objects. An adjoining grave, said to belong to a Gypsy Queen, for many years had a black purse on the stone which was said to be cursed and people would not touch.

Now along with the other townsfolk, Civil War soldiers, and area farmers there are the graves of several other gypsies. We will probably never know the full story of these "traveling people" but it's an interesting place and thought provoking.

Neosho

Now let's leave the tiny places and go to a really important place, Neosho. You didn't know that Neosho was so important? Read on.

You know all about the Pony Express don't you? It went from Independence to Sacramento. Our history books tell us all of the important details don't they? Maybe not. You see, on August 3, 1854 by special act of Congress a Pony Express mail route was established from Neosho to Albuquerque, New Mexico. This was just after the Mexican-American War so this region had come to be of great commercial and military importance but even so, the line was not a commercial success. In March of the following year the route was changed to run from Independence, Missouri to Stockton, California, via Albuquerque. The important thing is that Neosho was the original starting point for the Pony Express and this was six full years before the one we know about began its mail runs. Why don't our history books tell us about this one?

Neosho is a city of nicknames. It's first was "City of Springs" and that's a good one. In fact, the Osage word, "neosho" means it's a place of clear, cold water. The first settler in the area (1829) was Lunsford Oliver whose nearest neighbor was 60 miles to the east in Springfield. Of course more settlers came and in those early years the region was called "Six Bulls", a colloquialism of "six boils", referring to the big fast-flowing streams that flowed through the area.

Now Neosho likes to be known as "The Flower Box City" and that makes me think of George Washington Carver. The great plant scientist lived for a time in Neosho. The Flower Box City got its title back in 1957 after two years of work by the local Jaycees and others. Local lumber companies provided lumber at cost and the Jaycees built over 200 flower boxes. Pet Milk Co. donated 400 wooden barrels and the city fancied up trash cans and parking meters with flower baskets. Flower contagion spread and flower borders, flower gardens, and flower boxes are everywhere.

If you remember the old Dick Van Dyke Show, you will remember that Rob and Laura met at Camp Crowder where Dick was stationed. Well, Dick was truly stationed at Camp Crowder along with Carl Reiner, Mort Walker, Tillman Franks, and Jean Shepherd. When Mort Walker drew his Beetle Baily cartoons, he had Beetle stationed at a place called Camp Swampy which was his nickname for the soggy Camp Crowder.

There were some other surprising residents at Camp Crowder. You see, it was a Prisoner of War Camp for German prisoners during World War II. Did you know that Missouri had 30 POW camps? About all that remained of Camp Crowder when it was closed in 1951 was a group of fairly permanent buildings which formed the nucleus of the campus for the new Crowder College. The movie theater was taken apart and reassembled on the campus of the University of Missouri at Kansas City to become the Kansas City Playhouse.

While we're on the subject of military things, let's take a minute to think about the War Between the States. Missouri had 1,106 battles and skirmishes during that conflict so it's not surprising that a doozy of a battle took place in Neosho. But did you know that when Nathaniel Lyon expelled the Missouri Legislature from Jefferson City, some eventually went back but some went instead to Neosho. This town was Missouri's Confederate capital during the war.

Many stories are told of loot buried during the Civil War and people still enjoy looking for it. While doing my research for another book, I did find an article in The *Neosho Times* reporting that some boys were working for a farmer when they plowed up about $80 worth of gold and silver which the farmer had buried there at the beginning of the Civil War. The lost treasure, now found, was divided by the farmer as a reward for the honest boys. That was in 1878.

My favorite Neosho Times story however, was dated May 14, 1874. The *Times* reported, "A horse thief came to Pierce City on Tuesday. Result -- an empty saddle, an empty shot-gun and a new-made grave. They didn't say anything about Miranda Rights, years of litigation and appeals, book deals, or reality TV shows for the thief. He came to town on Tuesday and business was finished by the end of the day.

After the war a railroad came to Neosho and then, several more railroads and a fish hatchery opened there in 1888. Today that enterprise is known as the National Fish Hatchery and is the oldest Federal Fish Hatchery in the nation.

In 1882 the vineyards of Europe were dying because of a louse which killed the vines from the roots. You probably know that the native grape vines of Missouri were sent to Europe to be grafted to the vines existing there and therefore saved the wine industry in France, Germany, Italy, and the rest of Europe. What you may not know is that those grape stocks came by the thousands from Neosho. To be more precise, they came from the Monark Springs vineyards of Hermann Jaeger. Jaeger was later awarded the French Legion of Honour.

I've already mentioned some famous residents of Neosho and here are a few more. Thomas Hart Benton, the famous artist and muralist was born here. The Aviation pioneer, Hugh Armstrong Robinson was born in Neosho. He was the third person (after the two Wright brothers) to fly an airplane and the first person to make an air-sea rescue. He survived 15 crashes and died of natural causes at age 82. John Q. Hammons made millions in the hotel business and gave much of it to Missouri State University and other places. And yes, he also was from Neosho.

Besides this book, what else brings people to Neosho today? For sure, one is the Spooklight or Devil's Promenade just west of Neosho which attracts unknown numbers of curious visitors. A good map will show the little community of Hornet. That's the place to watch from and see the Spooklight on almost any night. Another big draw is the alternative energy industry. Neosho is the home to some of the best manufacturing operations for solar energy and wind energy. Crowder College is also involved in this.

When you put all of this together with Neosho's proximity to Branson, Springfield, Joplin, the Ozarks, and the Carver Monument, you have to wonder, "Why would anyone pass this by?"

McDonald County

While you're at Neosho, why not just drive the seven miles and cross the line into McDonald County? It's an interesting little place. (Little in terms of population.)

This is a place of resorts, bluffs, caves, and rivers and generally quiet and peaceful. But back in August of 1897 things weren't so quiet some folks rode into Pineville and robbed the McDonald County Bank. They got away with $589.23 and one man's pocket watch. The unusual thing about this robbery is that it featured 20-year-old Cora Hubbard in an active role. Female robbers were rare in those days.

Besides the natural beauty, McDonald County has two claims to fame. One is that Noel's post office is one of the busiest places anywhere at Christmas time. Everyone wants their Christmas cards to be postmarked, "Noel." The other is an event which happened in 1961 and demonstrates that Ozark-style good humor is in plentiful supply around here.

In 1961 the state's official tourism map had a glaring error. McDonald county had been left off! Now in a place that depends heavily on the tourist dollar, this was a major problem. Local businesses were bound to be hurt. So the area's leaders came up with a plan to generate much more interest than the map would have provided. They seceded from the state!

The county council summoned its representatives home from Jefferson City, prepared formal sounding speeches, seceded from the state, and formed McDonald Territory. They demonstrated their dissatisfaction with the state's lack of respect for their rural, isolated county.

They set up a provisional government, elected territorial officers, and printed their own tourism literature. A local Territorial Militia was formed and visas were issued. Vehicles entering the Territory were stopped by militiamen and, if the occupants were not local residents, they were given entry visas, local tourism information and directions to popular local places.

The Provisional Government of the Territory also established or licensed a private dispatch service, which provided mail service from the Territorial Post Office to the nearest U.S. Post Office. This private service issued a 2 cent stamp to charge for its services. Of course the stamps became big collector's items.

This writer remembers cleverly worded press releases coming from McDonald County on a regular basis. One hinted that the U.S.S.R. might be interested in opening a missile base there in the heart of the continent. Others announced that musical groups would perform at rallies and all sorts of fun events.

One person told me that the whole thing was stupid. I strongly disagree. I think that the McDonald County folks took a very real problem and handled it very effectively with humor. Did it work? We're still talking about it over fifty years later aren't we? How many publicity campaigns can claim anything like that?

Arrow Rock

. As with many Missouri cities and towns, Arrow Rock is clearly linked to Native American culture and activities. There is a cliff on the east end of the little town where the Indians went to find abundant flint rocks. They used these for making arrow heads. From this we get the name Arrow Rock. Even better, this place had salt licks (attracting game) and a dependable spring with fresh clean water. Lewis and Clark noted this place in their journals as they passed. A few years later westward-bound pioneers and explorers would stop at the spring. Eventually of course, some stayed and settled.

In 1821 William Becknell left this little settlement and went west all the way to Santa Fe. When he returned to the tavern in Arrow Rock with bags of silver and gold coins, the Santa Fe Trail was officially open. The town was not actually incorporated until 1829 and for its first four official years it was called Philadelphia. In 1833 they changed it back to Arrow Rock.

Many of the buildings, streets, gutters, etc. are from the mid-1800s so when you go, be sure to wear sturdy walking shoes. Turned ankles are a price you can pay for walking the very streets that the early giants did.

Speaking of early giants, in addition to Becknell and others who frequented this place, there were many important residents also. There were three 19th century governors; entrepreneur and medical doctor John Sappington, who was a pioneer in the treatment of malaria; and frontier artist George Caleb Bingham, who used Arrow Rock as the backdrop for some of his best known paintings.

The new Bucksnort Trading Post is now open. I know the owners well from their similar venture in Blackwater and I assure you that you will enjoy the unusual place. If you have the opportunity, you will also enjoy an old-fashioned production at the Lyceum.

It could certainly be said that Arrow Rock is a quiet little town. In fact, when they built their new jail in 1873 they proved it. You see, they only had one prisoner in there – ever. When his yelling kept the townspeople awake, they released him. But don't go to this place and think you can get rowdy. They'll still check you into a jail. It's just that it will be the one over in the county seat.

This writer recommends that you begin your Arrow Rock tour with the state's Visitors Center. The parking is plentiful and the restrooms are clean. There is a surprisingly good museum and the staff is courteous. Get the "Visitor's Guide" booklet to map out your many options. From there it's a short walk across the bridge into the 1800s.

Hermann

Hermann who? Lots of folks wonder that. Well Hermann wasn't named anyone with a last name. Actually it was named for a Teutonic warrior hero usually known as Armin or Arminius. That sounds a little like "Hermann" doesn't it? It must lose something in the translation. At any rate, Hermann was the Celtic leader who defeated Julius Caesar's Romans.

When the German settlers came to this area they started the new community and named it for the hero. They had big plans too. For instance, they made the town's main street ten feet wider than places like Philadelphia back east. These practical Germans were also fast to erect buildings of brick and stone. That's why the place, even today, has the look of a very old town and even something of a European look. This writer appreciates the way they keep up the old buildings and build new ones to match or blend with the old. That's the sort of thing that only happens when a community truly appreciates their heritage.

When most people think of Hermann they immediately think of beer and wine. That's both good and bad. Good in the sense that the area produces some of the world's best wine and has some pleasant bier gartens. The bad is because the place sometimes attracts too many young people who come to drink and lose control of themselves. Be aware that you may have problems during Mai Fest or October Fest that you would not have during other times of the year.

Street Scene in Hermann

So why visit at all? The reasons are limitless! First, this is as close to Germany as you can get without a plane ticket. German is still active as a second language. The museums and historic sites are filled with German items and thick with German atmosphere. The city is loaded with sites which are on the National Register of Historic Places. So many, in fact, that I can't list them all here.

As with Blackwater, I want to point out that this is not a theme park. It's a hard-working American small town with a wonderful heritage and people who value that.

If you enjoy wine or give it as gifts, visit the local wineries. Stone Hill is the most historic and most famous. It also may have some of the best scenery. However, there are many other good wineries in the vicinity and I don't think there's a bad one in the bunch. All types of dining is available too from picnics to nice little boutique cafes to fast foods to bier gartens. This writer suggests that for the best of the wurst, you should go to the Hermann Wurst Haus. It's a sausage shop/deli with indoor and outdoor seating.

Hermann is a terrific town for strolling and shopping. Not the upscale stuff but the antiques and other things you would expect in a small Midwestern town. They are one of the few small towns any more with bookstores and ice cream parlors, a concert shell, and a main street grocery. It's just a great place to stretch your legs in a pleasant safe environment for relaxing and casual dining.

So how do you really enjoy what Hermann has to offer? Well, that depends on how long you can stay. The longer you stay, the more "at home" you'll feel and the more you will enjoy the experience. If you can only stay for a short time, be sure to visit these two places. One is the Deutscheim State Historic

Site. Many people get caught up in the street life, beer gardens, wine tasting, and concerts and end up missing the best part of the town. I strongly urge you to visit the Deutcheim State Historic Site. This is the very best place to capture the heritage of German Americana in the 1850s. The other "must see" place is the Museum at the German School. It is all about life in early Hermann.

One final tip. While Amtrak is still a going concern, Hermann is a great ride from St. Louis or Kansas City or anywhere in between. Just relax and watch the scenery roll by. Grandkids will love it even more than you. Or, for the cyclists, don't forget about the Katy Trail access. If you're driving, you must go across the Missouri River on the new wide bridge and then come back to see the Hermann "skyline" from the river view. It's strikingly beautiful when seen from the north. The big U.C.C. Church and the ancient courthouse dominate and both buildings are unique. When you come off the bridge, there is a confusing intersection where you must pay attention to driving but, in that spot, is a tiny park with an impressive bronze statue of the old hero, Hermann, himself. What a wonderful destination is Hermann, Missouri!

Plato

What does Plato, Missouri have in common with Desperate Housewives? Nothing really but one of the shows screenwriters is from Plato. Another neat thing about this tiny town is its school. In one of my other books I wrote about what I learned at the Plato school even though I didn't attend there. That story was about the value of small town schools. I'm a real fan of small towns and small town schools because they do things so well.

There's almost nothing to see in Plato that you couldn't see somewhere else. However, right next door is Fort Leonard Wood and it's an interesting place where they do some amazing things with engineering and explosives. They also provide the basic training facilities for most of our nation's soldiers. A visit to the Military Museum at Fort Wood would be time well-spent.

The reason that I've included Plato in this book is that it has a distinction that no other place in the world can claim. The 2010 Census tells us that it is the population center of the United States. They have a marker and everything. It's just a stone's throw outside the town. So, the next time you're breezing down I-44 and need a break, take a side trip through Ft. Wood and Plato.

You Come From – Where?

Lots of people understand that Rolla was named after Sir Walter Raleigh but the people choosing the name just weren't sure about the spelling or even the pronunciation of the hero's name. So they filed the papers and the Ozarks' second largest city had its unique name. It's funny how these things happen but also it's funny how they take on lives of their own. In southwestern Kansas there is another town named Rolla – same spelling and everything. You guessed it – the town in Kansas was settled by folks from Rolla, Missouri. Even knowing this, I was still surprised to find a little town just a stone's throw from the Alaska Highway named Rolla, British Columbia. Sure enough, it was founded by settlers from Rolla, Missouri.

Many towns in Missouri were named for communities "back east" and, in times past, they just didn't worry too much about standardized spelling. The same is true for famous people like Raleigh and famous places like Madrid. So we see the possibility for some unusual names. Then we add our own pronunciations and – Well good luck with getting it right. My idea is that you do your best and always understand that you just can't please everyone.

One of my favorite town names is just a little community on the southwest side of Farmington. A man told me that he was from "Della Sue" and smiled when I wrote that. Then he informed me that the correct Spelling is DeLassus. That points up the fact that many people enjoy having strangers mispronounce or misunderstand their community's names.

Residents at Bois D'Ark are among those who seem to enjoy having you mispronounce the name of their hometown. The problem here comes from Frenchmen writing down the name used by Osage Indians. They were acknowledging the importance of the local hedge apple trees because the Natives liked using their wood to make bows. (A bow is a wooden arch, right?) Anyway the Ozarks English came along and the place name morphed into "BO-dark."

Most folks in Eastern Missouri just aren't certain how they should be saying the name of Berger. Well it sounds like "BUR-jer." Just off Interstate 44 in Franklin County is the little hamlet of Japan. That's an easy one of course. But don't be so sure. The locals say "JAY-pan." Further west on I-44 you will see the sign for Laquey. Everyone around Pulaski County knows that one is called "Lake Way."

When you're driving from Rolla to Licking you pass through Anutt. When the first postmaster decided to name the new community in honor of his daughter, he should have been a little more careful. He chose a pretty name for her, Anette, but his penmanship left something to be desired. So the officials in Jefferson City put it down as Anutt. The townsfolk decided to pronounce it as "a-NUT." Speaking of Licking, that town got its name because an important salt lick was located there. Any place where the deer were licking the ground was a good place for a settlement.

The western side of the state has some good names too. Eldorado Springs is pronounced in a very tentative way by many people. The locals say either "El-dough-RAY-dough Springs" or just plain "Eldo." The very French name of Versailles becomes something different in Missouri. Here, that place name became "Ver-SAILS." And Nevada (Nuh-VAH-duh) is a state but Missouri has "Nuh-VAY-duh."

Lebanon had a beautiful Osage name at one time. Settlers found the Native village of Wyota on that spot and continued to use that name for their town. Then they decided to name it Lebanon. To make matters worse, they call it "LEB-nun." A few miles away is a town named to honor The Great Liberator, Simon Bolivar. In Venezuela a person might actually hear him spinning in his grave as the Missourians say "BALL-uh-ver."

Cabool is named in honor of the capital city of Afghanistan, Kabul. For over 3,000 years it's been pronounced "KOB-el" but we say it like "Ku-BOOL." Everyone knows that in Missouri Hayti becomes "HAY-tie" and Paris is "PAIR-is." Our first capital city was New Madrid and I'm sure those Spanish settlers got it right. We, however, have changed it to "New MAH-drid." Not wanting to leave the Italians out of all this, let's remember that Missouri has Milan and we pronounce it "MY-lun."

Auxvasse is another French word and therefore another pronunciation problem. The name came from the nearby stream which was hard to cross. "Auxvasse" meant that it was easy for wagons to become mired in the stream's mud. At any rate, the little town which took its name from the troublesome creek has a name that makes people in Interstate 70 question themselves every time they pass the green and white signs. So here's the definitive answer. The town and the stream are pronounced "Of-AWS" or some might prefer "Of-OZ."

People on the Osage Reservation in Oklahoma will tell you that their tribe's name is actually *Wazhazhe*. With their nasal dialect, it may have sounded something like "Whu-SAHG-uh." The French came to Missouri and wrote the name as Osage and pronounced it as something like "Oh-SAHG" with a soft G. On the eastern side of the state the English-speakers heard the beginning of the word as something stronger and pronounced it more like "HOO-zahg" with the soft G. Eventually, to those folks, that became Huzzah with no G at all. The result is that Missourians have Osage County, the Osage River and much more. In the Ozarks they have the Huzzah River, Huzzah Creek, Huzzah Valley, and little community of Huzzah, Missouri.

In our cultural stewpot of Spanish, French, English, Native-American and more it's amazing that we can even agree on the pronunciation of our state's name. Of course, that is "Miz-ZOO-ree." Right?

Hornersville

You didn't think I was through talking about tiny towns, did you? If you know where Hornersville is, then you deserve some sort of geography prize. Now I have the folks in Lapland patting themselves on the back because they all know where it is. Where is Lapland? Well, that's what some folks in the Bootheel call their part of the state. It laps over into Arkansas, you see.

Back to Hornersville. Way down south of the throwed rolls and right at the Arkansas line is this little hamlet with one famous citizen. At least he's famous to those old enough to remember the early television commercials and shows like Howdy Doody. Out in the Hornersville Cemetery there is evidence of an unusual love story. The 20th century Romeo and Juliet are William "Major" Ray and his wife, Jennie.

Major erected a beautiful tombstone for his love. It is topped with a 37 inch angel with wings and everything. In fact it is a statue of his 37-inch-tall wife. Major's stone is next to hers. It has an image of himself and his dog. Major was the more famous one. He was 44 inches tall.

At one time Major and Jennie were stars of a circus which billed them as the smallest couple in the world but they left the circus life and opened a general store in Hornersville. One of the things they sold in that store was Buster Brown brand shoes. The St. Louis-based company advertised with boys they called Buster and his little dog named Tige. (Short for Tiger)

One day Major went to St. Louis and convinced the manufacturer that they were wasting their time employing a never-ending stream of little boys when they could instead hire a small man with show business experience. The advantage was that he wouldn't ever grow up. Of course they hired him and he went to work wearing boy's clothing and appearing on television with his dog. Do you remember the jingle? "I'm Buster Brown, I live in a shoe. Here's my dog Tige, He lives in there too." He encouraged us to look for his picture in the shoe before we would buy it.

Something else you should know about that store: Major and Jennie had a business partner. He was an old and valuable friend from their circus days. In fact he was the giant from the circus, Shadrick Archibald Shields (a.k.a. Shade Shields at 6 feet 8 inches). Can you imagine walking into a little general store in a tiny town and finding the clerks were the world's smallest couple and a giant?

So, when you're in the Bootheel, swing by Hornersville and see the monuments for two small people with a big big love. After you finish this book you might like to read *For the Love of Jennie* by Laura Ford. It's a story of this great love, of Jennie and Major Ray, and the little dog, Tige. These little people had some amazing adventures back in the 1890s and in the early twentieth century.

The Village

This time let's see if you can tell me what town I describing. In the last census an unusual place was described. This little community likes to call itself a village rather than a town or city. As of a recent Census, there were 140 people, 82 housing units with 81 households, and only 19 families residing in the village. What?

Only 2½% of the households have children. Less than 4% of the households have no husband but over 76% of the households were non-families. The average household size was just over one person. The average family size was just over two people. None of the families in this village live below the poverty line.

This tiny village has a skyscraper which is visible from a wide area southwest of Kansas City. I'll bet you have figured out now what I've been describing. This little community is Unity Village in Jackson County. It is sort of like the Vatican for the Unity Church. Do you want to visit there? I don't know if you do or not, but now you will know what you're seeing from several area highways.

GIANTS AMONG US

Massive Maxie, the Hefty Honker

When next time you're around Chariton County, you should visit two small towns to see two very large things. Sumner likes to call itself the Goose Capital of the World. They refer to the Canada goose which migrates through the area and provides great opportunities for hunters. Each year this little town (population 142) sponsors a festival to celebrate the goose and in 1976, as they crowned the Goose Queen, a truly remarkable bird flew in

Her name was **Maxie**. (The goose – not the queen.) She stands 40 feet tall and has a wingspan of 61 feet and weighs over 4000 pounds. And, yes, I did say that the big goose flew in to Sumner's park. To be more accurate, she was flying with the help of a lifting helicopter.

Now wouldn't you think that a big fiberglass sculpture with outstretched 61 foot wings would have problems with the wind on the open prairie? Not Maxie! She swivels and turns to always face into the wind and that way is very aerodynamic.

GIANTS AMONG US

(CONT.)

As they say on TV, "But wait – There's more!" Just a few miles from where you stand in Sumner there is another gigantic creation. Back in 1947 George James discovered an especially tasty type of **pecan** growing right there on his property near Brunswick. Its popularity grew and the James family prospered. So, in 1982, they created a huge concrete pecan and set it out for the world to see.

The creation used to be seen in front of the Nut Hut roadside stand on Highway 24, which is the location of the James' home. In 2013, however, it was moved to its new home in beautiful downtown Brunswick. It weighs 12,000 pounds and is twelve feet long or tall or whatever you would call its biggest dimension. Lots of other folks in the area now harvest pecans and yes, there is a Pecan Festival each October.

The Ponderous and Prodigious Pecan

GIANTS AMONG US

I'm not imaginative enough to dream this stuff up. These things really exist. On Highway 107 east of Stoutsville there is a **giant chigger**. It's at a place called Chigger Hill. Nevada, MO has a giant **morel mushroom** 30 feet tall. At Henry Coffer's barber shop in Charleston you can find the world's largest **ball of human hair**. At this writing it weighs 167 pounds. Salisbury's claim to fame is the pair of giant metal **grasshoppers** on Highway 24.

Right at the state line in Seneca you can see the world's largest **Milnot can**. Jefferson City has a big **pacifier** made of cigarette butts. This one requires a lot of maintenance and may not be there long. As you drive down 36th Street in St. Joe. you will see a building that looks like a **giant pink ice cream cone.** It's a terrific, well-run place and worth stopping. Tipton has a giant eight ball which doubles as their water tower.

Branson has a **giant banjo** in the Grand Country Square. This one is a true giant as its neck alone is 47 feet long. It's too big for the building so it sticks out through a window and reaches toward the street. Webb City has a set of giant **hands in prayer** and Weston has the largest **ball of string.**

GIANTS AMONG US

(CONT.)

One of my favorites is the **giant bullfrog** known as W. H. Croaker. It's right on old Route 66 in Waynesville. A local art teacher painted the limestone outcropping one day and local students have kept the stony amphibian painted ever since. It's just silliness but things like this make the world more fun and interesting.

W. H. Croaker

GIANTS AMONG US

At the Nelson-Atkins Art Museum in Kansas City they have giant **shuttlecocks** on the lawn. (A shuttlecock is that birdie that you hit when you play badminton.) Each birdie is eighteen feet tall and weighs 2.5 tons. At the Kemper Museum of Contemporary Art there is a gigantic spider maybe ten (?) feet tall. There is a library on West 10th Street which appears to be a row of **gigantic books** one block long. Each book is 25 feet high. At 404 Eighth Street (downtown) there is about a **20 foot needle** sticking through a big red button. At 1219 Union, look up. You'll see the world's largest **cap gun**. And at the Western Missouri Soccer League fields you will find the world's largest concrete **soccer ball.**

On the other side of the state in St. Louis, there is a huge **Indian** at the Cherokee Street neighborhood's antique row. It's so ugly that even the sculptor doesn't like it. Turtle Park across from the Zoo has several **giant turtles** for the kids to climb on. The Sappington Farmers Market has a **giant farmer** with his giant son. Downtown on Eighth Street there is a **giant's head**. It's so big you can walk around inside and peek out of its eyes. Even bigger are the **teeth** at the Dental Health Theater on Laclede's Landing. Downtown Clayton has a super-sized shoe which happens to be constructed of shoes. Laumeier Sculpture Park in Sunset Hills has a genuinely creepy work of wonderful "art." The 12 foot **eyeball** called the *Eye* is a sculpture on display within the free

GIANTS AMONG US

(CONT.)

You will find a super-sized **caterpillar and butterfly** out in Chesterfield at the Faust Park. They are at the entrance to the Missouri Botanical Garden's Butterfly House. Also in Chesterfield is *The Awakening*. This sculpture is also 70 feet long and 17 feet tall. It looks like a giant is waking and coming up out of the ground.

But Wait – There's More! I had been driving right past an attraction near I-44 for several years but never stopping to see it. Big mistake! Right out there beside Highway ZZ (old Route 66) in Fanning, MO is the world's largest **rocking chair**. This Paul Bunyan type of furniture stands as tall as a four story building and it actually measures up to its hype. Yes it is a world record item. If you plan ahead and visit in August, the local fire department brings a hoist truck and lifts people up into the seat.

And even more! Behind the Idea Center on Chesterfield in Springfield is a gleaming **35 foot fork**. Finally, it's with sadness that I make a revision in this new edition. In the old edition, I described at this point the world's largest **paper cup**. It has stood in place on Glenstone Avenue in Springfield for many decades but is now nothing more than nostalgia.

Food Challenges

There are some wonderful places in Missouri to get some wonderful meals. There are also some wonderful places to totally pig out. We know about Lambert's and how no one can leave hungry. There are lots of "all you can eat" places but I'm talking now about something way beyond those places. There are some places where they serve you an especially good meal and challenge you to eat it. If you eat it all, it's free! Be warned that these contests come and go even faster than restaurants open and change and close. Call ahead before you go.

Mama Campisi's in **St. Louis** will serve you a big bowl of spaghetti and marina sauce and one meatball. If you can eat it, it's free and you get a shirt and other recognition. Here's the deal however. There's a lot of spaghetti but that meatball is bigger than a softball. For a little over $20.00 it might be worth a try.

There's a Pizza place in **Richmond Heights** called Pointers. They serve a 28 inch, ten pound pizza with either two meat toppings or four vegetable toppings. You have one hour to eat the thing and, if you do, you get $500.00 and there are other rewards too! Now here's the good part of this one. It's a contest for two! Yes, you get help with this one. There have been several winners from across the country so it can be done. There are rules such as it is only done on Wednesdays at 3:00. So check in advance.

Food Challenges (cont.)

This one you have to know about in advance. It's not well-publicized. At the **Doolittle** exit on I-44 and right on old Route 66 there's a nice little restaurant called Cookin' From Scratch. This place serves a 66 ounce burger on a 1¼ pound bun with all the trimmings. You also get 1½ pounds of French fries. (You lucky thing, you!) If you can finish this little snack in 66 minutes or less, you pay nothing. Ambulance and medical bills may be extra. This challenge has been successfully met. Will you be next?

In **Blue Springs** there's a family restaurant named Betty's Burgers. Betty offers a challenge to eat a five pound hamburger along with three pounds of French fries. If you can do it in under an hour, it's free. Still hungry? Well right there in Blue Springs you can go over to Yugurtini and try to eat 30 oz. of yogurt in 30 minutes. If you can do it, you get a free tee shirt. You should probably get a size 4-X Large.

You might like to try Mario's Italian Grill in **Bonne Terre**. They have a 28 inch pizza challenge which will be free if you and one friend can eat the thing on the spot. Check with them ahead of time about times and conditions.

Food Challenges (cont.)

Branson is famous for many things but, until now, it was not known for pigs. Why not start your Branson vacation with some Hell Fire Chili at Tijuana Willie's? All you have to do is eat a bowl of this particular chili and wait five minutes before taking a drink of anything. Don't like chili? Then Willie offers a contest to see if you can down their 7 pound burrito in one sitting. Then, to finish your dining experience, you could go to Montana Mike's Steakhouse and see if you're up to a 44 oz. sirloin steak at Montana Mike's Steakhouse. What's for dessert?

The Almost Famous Grille & Barbeque in **West Plains** has a 2 pound burger they call the Daddy Sasquatch. If you finish it on the spot, you get a free tee shirt.

Go to Holland Café and Meats in **Fenton** if you want to try their 72 oz. steak challenge. Along with the four-and-a-half pounds of flesh you must eat 8 butterfly shrimp, a salad, a baked potato, a roll and a drink. If you do, it's free and you are certifiably insane.

In **Bogard**, you might like to try Pin Oak Hill for the Hot Wing Challenge. On Thursdays, they offer eight spicy wings to eat as fast as you can. If you set a record, you get a tee shirt.

Food Challenges (cont.)

You can win $200 or more in **Bolivar** if you can eat the five pound burger at Mister Wings. If you fail, you can try again and the cash prize the next time will be even bigger.

There's a 20 minute challenge at the Steamboat Café in **Hannibal**. If you can eat the six pound pancake that quickly – no charge!

The Lee Street Deli in **Columbia** has a novel idea. If you can win their eating contest, they give you more food. The Wall of Fame Challenge beckons you to eat eight spicy burgers in one sitting. The prizes are another burger and a tee shirt. From there you can go over to the Stadium Grill and try their 6 ½ pound burger challenge. All you have to do is eat that along with 2 pounds of fries and you get $600.00. That will come in handy to pay for your hospital bills.

Do you like dining for cash? In **Chesterfield**, Talyna's has a Monster Manhattan Style Pizza Challenge. If you can eat this 30 inch monster and consume two pitchers of soda, you get $2000.00.

Food Challenges (cont.)

Let's go to **Hallsville** and the Bad Citizen Coffee shop. They have the Bad Citizen Meal Challenge which is a triple-decker burger along with chili cheese fries. Chomp it all down in thirty minutes or less and you get another burger! By the way, would you brag to your friends that you won the Bad Citizen Challenge?

The Buckin' Bull Saloon in **Canton** offers a three-pound burger that's free if you can eat it in one sitting. If that's not enough of a challenge, then go to **Salem** where the Scotzilla Burger awaits. If you can eat this 5 pound giant in one sitting, it's yours along with a tee shirt to remember your victory.

There are breakfast challenges too. The nice Carraige House Restaurant in **Springfield** is a traditional family place. But it offers the World's Biggest Omelot. It's made with 15 eggs, green peppers, ham, onions, chopped tomatoes, bacon, and sausage. Put that with a double order of hashbrowns and you have a real breakfast! It's free if you can finish it off in less than 30 minutes.

Food Challenges (cont.)

The breakfast at the Midway Travel Plaza in **Midway**, MO has even been on national TV. Their challenge is called The Big 70. It has seven breakfast bisquits covered with 70 ounces of sausage gravy. It's your if you can eat it and it has been done before.

I don't know why the TV crew went to Midway. They probably should have gone to **Kansas City** for a breakfast challenge. There's a Pancake Wall of Fame at the City Diner where they honor people who can really put 'em away. The record for eating these giant pancakes is six and it is held by a seventy year old man and a seven year old girl

Finally, still in **Kansas City**, there is a place called Succotash. Here you can find the Sumo Challenge. It's just a nice pancake breakfast but it also has three eggs, peppers, onions, and home fries. Its total weight is nine pounds! It's free if you can eat it in one sitting.

Hamilton

Let's start with what everybody already knows about Hamilton. First, J.C. Penney grew up there. Second, he started his first store there. Third, he moved away to New York and never looked back. OK, the first one was right. But that part about his first store is way off. There actually was a J.C. Penney store in Hamilton but it was his 500th Penney location. And the third part is very wrong. He returned to Missouri and stayed at his farm near Hamilton (actually nearer to Nettleton) as often as he possibly could.

He was often seen by the locals wearing his bib overalls and driving around the gravel roads in his little Chevy coupe. Waving as he went past was often not good enough. Penney took many opportunities to stop and maintain old acquaintances along the farm roads and in Hamilton's little cafes. He loved his friends, his angus cattle, and dining at the nearby McDonald's Teahouse with Joyce Hall (Hallmark Cards) and others.

What else does everyone know? Well, of course, Hamilton is a sleepy little farm town where nothing interesting ever happens. This one is also very wrong! Let's look back a little. In the early days there was only the prairie, grazing animals, their predators, and the wildlife associated with the area's meandering rivers. Then two towns grew up on opposite sides of the state and competed with each other to be Missouri's second largest cities.

Hannibal and St. Joseph were river towns and the great rivers provided for their needs. Connecting them seemed an important thing to do and the prairie provided no major obstacles except for places where the rivers might be forded. So eventually a trail was laid out and stage coaches were running a regular schedule along this Hound Dog Trail. They were accompanied by folks on horseback and in various kinds of wagons.

In the mid-1800s, John Clemens (father of Samuel L. Clemens) and others decided that a railroad connecting the two growing communities would be a great business opportunity. Eventually they created the Hannibal-St. Joseph Railroad and it was an instant success. This railroad was the reason that St. Joseph was chosen as the terminus for the Pony Express. You see, the train brought the mail to St. Joe and there, it was put on fast ponies for the rest of trip to California.

It was at this time that the Irish were flooding into America and many of them went straight to the hiring offices in Hannibal where they signed on to lay the tracks and construct small depots all along the way. They earned good wages but had few opportunities to spend their money. The railroad supplied sleeping quarters and food so their wages accumulated into large savings. Then the job was done and the railroad offered the land along the right-of-way to those "Railroad Irish"

The Railroad Irish had their dream of wonderful American farm land and the railroad itself had a built-in customer base. Both groups prospered. And that is how many Missouri communities, including Hamilton, came to be. Honest, hard-working people, many of them Catholic, have left their mark on this part of the state.

Eventually U.S. Highway 36 was built from Ohio to Colorado and much of the road paralleled the Hannibal & St. Joe Railroad. Today this road has been nicknamed the Way of American Genius because of the many great people and ideas which have sprung up in its path. Hannibal gave us the literary genius of Samuel Clemens. Laclede gave us the military genius of General John J. (Black Jack) Pershing, Chillicothe gave the world commercial sliced bread. Marceline gave us the creative genius of the inventor of animated cartoons and theme parks, Walt Disney. Hamilton gave entrepreneurial retail genius of James Cash Penney. The broadcast and entertainment genius coming from St. Joseph included Ralph D. Foster, Jane Wyman, and Walter Cronkite among many others.

Then, for whatever reason, the nice little town of Hamilton began to experience hard times. Finances toughened for the farmers, retailers struggled and eventually gave up. When the J.C. Penney store closed its doors, everyone knew the end had come. The empty shell of a pleasant little town baked in the prairie sun and wind. Although an exaggeration, it was called by some, a ghost town.

Then Sarah Gailbraith and Jenny Doan shook up the little town of 1,800. They started something known as the Missouri Star Quilt Company and things have never been the same. At this writing, no less than fifteen buildings have been remodeled, painted, and filled with fabrics, sewing machines, learning centers and customers from all over the United States and beyond.

Just as J.C. Penney used his device of "Golden Rule" pricing, Jenny Doan uses her device (YouTube) to pass the word about quilting and about her operation in Hamilton which has become the Quilting Mecca. You might be interested to know that the family has put in an area known as "Man's Land" which will give husbands and boyfriends something to do while they wait. Thank you!!! At this writing, the name was still being chosen but it's right there in the middle of everything and I can guarantee that it will be a popular spot.

Men looking for something to do might also see just where all of the busses have come from and do a quick check of the license plates up and down Davis Street. (a.k.a. the main drag, a.k.a. Highway 13) It's truly amazing to see just where these quilters are from. This place now reminds me in some ways of the tourist Mecca known as Wall Drug in South Dakota but there is a huge difference. At Wall Drug, people are pulling off the highway to see what it's like and maybe grab a bite or a souvenir and then be gone. It's not really a destination in itself. At Hamilton, the folks are arriving on a mission. They are quilters who come to learn and to supply themselves for their hobby. They stay. They spend!

Those quilters are on a pleasant mission and the Missouri Star employees are extremely courteous and friendly. It all makes for a happy atmosphere and a very pleasant place to visit even if you don't quilt. Add indoor and outdoor restaurants, shady sidewalks, and you have an enjoyable destination. But there is even one more attraction that I should mention. Right there on Davis Street is a free air-conditioned museum about the life of J.C. Penney. It's in the new library building.

One of the main centers of activity at the Missouri Star Quilt Company is the old store on the corner that used to be the J.C. Penney store. I feel quite certain that Mr. Penney would be delighted with its resurrection. A smile came on this writer's face as I walked into that store and found that the old hardwood floors still squeak. That loud squeaking was one of my favorite memories of the old building. Some things should never change.

Being a Good Guest

In composing my thoughts about Hamilton, I was reminded of many things from a time when I was a frequent visitor in the town. They had two small cafes in those days and both were good places for a nice meat and potatoes type of meal. Desserts were also consistently good. If you went there in the morning on almost any day other than Sunday you would meet a group of older men, mostly retired farmers who would get together over a cup of fresh coffee and solve the world's problems. That's one of the nicest things about many small towns across the Midwest.

However, there was a time of trouble. The men would often get a cup of coffee and, when that was dry, they expected free refills. Good conversations might go on for hours while the men talked and sipped. This was usually fine because they were nice guys and the staff could continue to work at preparing for the lunch and dinner crowds. Then the conversations began to extend past 11:00 or even noon. Lunch customers would show up but find no place to sit. Soon, they stopped coming.

When the restaurant owners brought the problem to the attention of the old men, the men were angry. "After all, we're your best customers," they said. "We come here every day and you don't even appreciate us."

Earlier I wrote about what I wished some communities would do to be more welcoming to visitors. Customers can also be more considerate of their hosts. Spending fifty cents for a cup of coffee does not make it right for us to crowd out other paying customers. When we think about it there are many ways that we can be better guests in communities where we visit. We should also be teaching consideration to the children and grandchildren who may be traveling with us.

Here are some visitor behaviors that make me grit my teeth:

- Talking so loudly that other people are forced to hear every word you say. You're not that entertaining.

- Using restrooms without making any purchase.

- Leaving a mess in the restroom for someone else to -- clean up.

- Taking two parking spaces on busy parking lots.

- Profanity – No one is impressed.

- "Stiffing" a waiter or waitress. It's not funny and no one is laughing about it.

- Letting your child scream and misbehave. They're not learning to do better unless you're doing some teaching. Make them want to do better. When I reached a certain age, my father used to say, "I can't make you do the right thing but I can make you wish you had." And I knew he meant it.

- Throwing ice chips, food, or other items. Slippery spots on floors and sidewalks are not funny.

- Pretending to be more sophisticated than your hosts or treating them with condescension. They may know aspects of life that you will never understand. Treating others with respect brings a mirrored treatment back to you.

- Treating older people with condescension. They absolutely definitely know aspects of life that you will never understand. Treating others with respect brings a mirrored treatment back to you. Learn from them.

- Littering anyone's home town.

- Speeding or ignoring anyone's local rules of the road. These can all be summed up with the Golden Rule. It applies no matter where you might live or be visiting.

Kimmswick

I need to start at the beginning on this town. It began with <u>Theodore Kimm</u> a German-born merchant who found success in St. Louis and in 1859 bought a tract of land in Jefferson County which he developed into a new community. He was from Brunswick in Germany and he seems to have combined his own name with that of his birthplace in creating the name Kimmswick. Some will say that the "wick" part denotes a small hamlet or village. Others say that it indicates the nearness of a salt lick. I'll bet that he had a combination of the three in mind.

Back in the 1700s the traffic in Missouri was almost completely by river. Then the residents built what they called El Camino Real which means something like The Royal Highway. It went from the Spanish territorial capital at New Madrid and up through Ste. Genevieve, all the way to St. Louis. The Missouri Daughters of the American Revolution placed a large stone to mark the site of this old road. You can see it about 30 feet back from <u>Highway K</u> just before you enter Kimmswick. It's right on the bank of <u>Rock Creek</u>. Stop for a minute and imagine ox carts with two gigantic wooden wheels lumbering up and down this muddy trail.

This must have been a beautiful place in those days with magnificent virgin oak and other forest giants all along the way. In 1807 Meriwether Lewis was the territory's governor and he and the Legislature ordered an improvement of the El Camino Real (called Rue Royale by the French). They removed trees and increased the width of the road to 25 feet.

1858 was an important year for this area. The St. Louis Iron Mountain and Southern Railroad came through and brought settlers and speculators with it. Remember, Theodore Kimm established the town the next year. Soon there were farmers, stores, a grist mill, an iron forge, and a brewery. A limestone quarry was shipping its products on the railroad. There was even a greenhouse sending fresh flowers to St. Louis on the train each day.

Soon a wide variety of businesses were operating and three schools were at work. The St. Joseph Catholic School was one of those and it is still educating children today! The now wealthy Mr. Kimm donated many parcels of land for use as a city park, a cemetery, and more. In 1876 he buried his wife in that cemetery. He went on to travel the world and made 29 crossings of the Atlantic. Finally he died in Switzerland in 1886.

For a long time in the 1800s Kimmswick was a destination for day-tripping St. Louisans who would ride the train or the steamboats to visit the Montesano Springs Park and drink the mineral waters. This big amusement park had 14 springs which supplied a large bottling industry and sent shipments of water to many American cities and towns.

Once again let's stop and imagine this little village with its beer gardens, brass band, gaslights, and prosperous shops. All of these supported by streams of visitors arriving daily by railroad coach and steamboat. Then problems arrived in the form of the automobile.

Kimmswick was having troubles by 1917 when they established their first speeding ordinances with a limit of eight miles per hour. Within a month a reward was being offered for information on the person(s) who tore down the speed limit signs. In spite of feelings about the auto nuisance, it was still the preferred method of transportation and by 1927 all of the horse's hitching posts and watering troughs had been removed.

The major problem, however, was not the occasional automobile but the steady stream of cars whose owners were demanding improved roadways. New highways were constructed west of the town and the steamboats and passenger trains no longer came. Kimmswick was not a destination point any longer but just a little spot to speed by. Savvy business owners fled the town and moved over next to the highway. Kimmswick was not dead but it was basically forgotten.

Then, to the rescue, came Lucianna Gladney-Ross. It was her idea to restore the town to something of its former glory. In 1970 the townsfolk began a project to restore several homes and then more and then more. Today between Second, Elm, Third, and Oak Streets you can see much of what they accomplished. Many old log buildings from the area have been dismantled and reassembled for you. There are now forty four buildings in this little hamlet which are listed on the National Register of Historic Places. The Old House Steak House is one of those and it is still operating every day.

The Old Steak House

So far I've told you about the unique history of this little hamlet in Jefferson County but why would you want to go today? What will you find? You will be surrounded by well-maintained old stores and homes – all in red brick or tastefully painted earth tone colors. You will find wonderful dining in several places including the Blue Owl. This restaurant and bakery features the three S's, soup, salad, and sandwiches but they are nationally famous for their deserts. The Levee High Apple Pie (made with eighteen apples!) has been featured on national TV and in National magazines several times recently.

Those pesky automobiles will still get you to Kimmswick if you are willing to get off the main highway for a minute. You will have to look closely for the Highway K sign on Highway 67. The town has, in fact, now embraced the automobile and has a classic auto show each Father's Day.

In the olden times you could arrive by riverboat and you still can! For just a few times each year you can get on the Tom Sawyer in St. Louis for the riverboat trip downstream and a bus ride back to the Arch. It's a little pricey but you do get a lunch at the Blue Owl. You must have reservations for this so call (877) 982-1410 toll-free in advance.

Remember this place only has 150 residents but they still host a tribute to veterans on every Memorial Day weekend, the Strawberry Festival every June, and the Apple Butter

Festival which draws over 100,000 people over two days in late October. A crowd of 100,000 is not my style but obviously, lots of people do enjoy it. It's like Yogi told us, "It's so crowded, nobody comes here anymore."

What is my style is the Christmas season in Kimmswick. They have their streets lined with luminaries and the shops are open late. The decorations are tasteful and the atmosphere is very traditional. At Christmas time they do a cookie walk that's lots of fun.

What more could 150 residents do? Well, I don't think they should try. What they do now is something very special and why mess with a good thing? This is in Jefferson County after all so there are plenty of services available and I really think you should plan to spend all day here. If you don't, you will just find yourself wanting to come back anyway. Kimmswick has been named as one of the best small towns in the Midwest and I think they richly deserve that recognition.

Mastodons

Just a note to remind you that if you are visiting Kimmswick, you are just a stone's throw away from the Mastodon State Historic Site. It's a small place just on the other side of Interstate 55 from Kimmswick so it will only take a short time to see what they have to offer. You will be glad you stopped.

This is the exact site where they dug the mastodon bones out of the ground and you can still see the digs. In addition they have other bones such as the giant ground sloth and the saber-tooth cat. (Popularly called saber-tooth tiger.) These reassembled life-sized giants are something you won't soon forget. Missouri's state parks and sites are all good and most are quite wonderful. Take advantage of these gems whenever you can. Small children are free and adults are $4.00.

Carthage

Carthage is a terrific town which is often overshadowed by its bigger sisters, Joplin and Springfield. It is known for its troubled history during the War Between the States and for its fine quality limestone. This can be quarried and polished into what people call Carthage Marble. Most people are familiar with Carthage marble which was used to build our state's capitol building.

Thanks to the railroads, there are many other good examples of this stone in buildings across the nation. One outstanding example is in the middle of Carthage. The Jasper County Courthouse is probably Missouri's most beautiful. It's worth going a little out of your way just to see this impressive building.

From the end of the Civil War onward Carthage has been a prosperous place and the old Victorian-style homes show good evidence of that. The Carthage South District which contains many of these homes is now on the National Register of Historic Places. Speaking of wealth, it's very unusual for a city this small to be home to a Fortune 500 company but Carthage is. Leggett & Platt has been there since 1883.

Many food producing corporations also call Carthage home. The left-overs from the food processing are used by Renewable Environment Solutions to produce energy in their thermal conversion plant.

Another unique feature of Carthage is the large number of Vietnamese Catholic immigrants who have settled in the town. These folks have a celebration each year called Marian Days which draws from 50,000 to 70,000 visitors.

Now why do tourists come to Carthage today? I'm sure that the number one reason is to see the Precious Moments Park and Chapel. Another big draw is to walk among the Victorian homes in the Carthage South District. Most people will want to see the statue of Marlin Perkins. This was the home of the Director of the St. Louis Zoo and the host for two decades of television's Wild Kingdom. Do you remember Marlin saying things like, "Just look at Jim wrestle that python! Do you need help, Jim?" Perkins was always smart enough to have his assistant do the wrestling, wasn't he?

Others, no doubt, flock to see the Carthage version of a crop dusting aircraft. Mounted on a pole high above the street, this "aircraft" doesn't really spray crops in the typical way. You see, its body is a manure spreader so locals call it the crap duster. Also high in the air in another part of Carthage is an old Chevy pickup truck with the driver lounging inside while his wife(?) is outside changing the tire.

But I've saved the best for last. A well-known collector, Lowell Davis, has bought an entire 1929 era town and moved it to his property. I used the word entire because he has everything there that you might imagine. He can hang out in his own private town but he also likes to share with people who stop by. I know what you're thinking but he doesn't charge an admission price at all. How do you find Lowell's place and the town of Red Oak II? Follow the Burma-Shave signs. How cool is that?

Fort Osage

     This one is very hard to find but worth the effort in every way. Let's say that you've been in Independence and you've already seen the Truman Home, the Presidential Library, the Log Courthouse and Leila's Hair Museum. Now you're ready to drive westward on Highway 24 to Buckner. Notice the barbeque place in Buckner for future reference. You will want to come back.

     In Buckner you will turn north on Sibley Street which is Highway BB. Watch carefully for directional signs and after about 3 miles you will arrive at a very special place. The town of Sibley and the trading post called Fort Osage are yours for the day.

     When Lewis and Clark went west in 1804, Clark wrote in his journal about a place on a steep hill about 70 feet above the Missouri River. He thought it would be a perfect place for a trading post or a military fort. Later, when he was Governor of the Territory, Congress directed him to set up a trading post and try to make friends with the Osage and other Indian nations. He already knew just the place.

He asked the businessman, George Sibley, to run the trading post and he arranged for a military unit to be deployed to construct and defend the place. Clark and Sibley went upstream and established this enterprise in 1808. In addition to this becoming a major instrument for improving Indian and white American's relations, it also brought the Native Americans into a lasting partnership with us instead of the British or the French who were trying to do the same thing. This little place was crucial to the opening of the west.

Clark returned to St. Louis but Sibley and his wife, Mary, stayed in the western part of Missouri for a long time. Eventually Sibley was asked to survey the Santa Fe Trail and to do many other things for Congress. In their later years George and Mary returned to their home in the St. Charles area. It was a large estate with many linden trees and they called it Linden Wood. Mary started a school there which became Lindenwood University.

The soldiers were called to duty in the War of 1812 and the trading post was closed. It re-opened for a time but then was finally abandoned. Settlers who eventually came to the area were delighted to find all of the timber already cut and trimmed so they took the place apart to build their houses and outbuildings.

Now the good news. Plenty of traces remained of the fort's structure and Clark's plans and drawings were very complete so Jackson County rebuilt the facility just the way it was 200 years ago. It is now a county park staffed by people in period costumes and those folks are very knowledgeable and helpful. I wish that every Missourian could visit this place. I certainly hope that you will.

Fort Osage

If you visit, you might want to avoid the early part of the day in April and May. This place is full of kids on field trips! One time that you might like in spite of the small crowds is in September. The weather is pleasant and they host the **Grand Festival of Chez les Canses.** It celebrates the early European settlement that became Kansas City. Visitors can compare and contrast clothing, shelters and tools from various early settler groups during the two-day festival. They play 18th century live music and even have what they call a "period-appropriate" church service on Sunday morning. There is a small charge with discounts for children and seniors.

California

    If you should find yourself somewhere between Lupus, Enen, McGirk, and Kliever, you should probably swing over to Burger's Smokehouse for lunch. It's more than a typical smokehouse, you see. It's just the place to get that ground buffalo that you've been craving. Or how about some frog legs or burnt ends? Take the burnt ends home for your baked beans and you'll never want beans any other way.

    But this smokehouse-turned-deli has something else that is unique. It has a visitors center with two-story wildlife dioramas, murals, a working water-wheel, and even a little theater to tell you about the history of the place. It's not your average butcher shop. You <u>will</u> be amazed at the size of this place.

    This is in California which is the county seat of Moniteau County. And it's not really as isolated as I made it sound. It's right on a major coast-to-coast highway (Highway 50) and it's located between Jefferson City and Sedalia. California has more to offer than just a great deli. Did you know that your Honeysuckle turkeys come from California? Originally known as Boonsborough, the Post Office said it needed a different name because Missouri already had a Boonsborough. The story is that a man named California Wilson bribed the name selection committee with two gallons of whiskey and that's how the town got its name. That was back in 1848.

They built a very handsome and unique courthouse in 1867 and that's the one that you still see there today. There is a nice museum on the entire first floor of that building. While you're there look around and check out some other significant buildings including the old Finke Opera House/Ritz Theatre, the Eitzen Mansion, the Gray-Wood Buildings and the Cultural Heritage Center.

There are other reasons to visit California. The Moniteau County Fair began in 1866 and is believed to be the oldest continuous fair west of the Mississippi. The products of local gardens always show up at a fair. It's still a good one too. Right now California's champion gardener is Amber Traschel who, while still a fourth grader was earning scholarship money by growing her produce including a 36 pound cabbage There is also a hare and hounds balloon race on the third Saturday of every July. Hot air balloons are always fun to be around and a great opportunity to take some bright cheerful pictures.

One last item to make you think about California any time you're driving down a Missouri roadway. Have you seen those huge orange balls on the power lines? They are put there to warn low-flying aircraft about the lines. Well, they all come from California, Missouri. There's a good trivia item to impress your friends!

Milan

Originally known as Pharsalia Post Office, this little place needed a name change. Pharsalia was too hard to pronounce. So the townsfolk decided, back in 1844, to change the name to Milan. They pronounce it MY-lun. If you're traveling on Route 5 or Route 6, you might want to stop and pay your respects at the local cemetery.

Pete Kibble's foot is buried there. Pete was a local guy who lost his foot in a railroad accident. He had the foot buried in Oakwood Cemetery, under a marker that reads, "Pete Kibble's Foot 1917." He did that so he would have a grave available and someday, when the rest of him died, he could be reunited with his foot. But then Pete had a change of heart and went out to the wild west never to return. As a result, there remains in Milan's Oakwood Cemetery a grave clearly marked as Pete Kibble's Foot. If you travel the world, how many things like that will you see?

Fulton

Enough foolishness! Let's talk about some important stuff. This town has an important history going way back to a time just after the Lewis and Clark Expedition came through. It was founded in 1808. It is the biggest city in Callaway County which was named for James Callaway. The Callaways were friends and relatives of the Boones and had come with old Dan'l from Kentucky.

In 1861, Colonel Jefferson Jones got word that the Union forces were nearby. He mustered his "troops" and rode out to meet them at the county line. Arriving early the Callaway County men cut trees and placed the logs to look like cannon and set lots of small "campfires" to give the impression of a large force. The Union troops agreed to stay out of Callaway County if Jones' troops would keep the peace and not support the South. The county stayed safe and free of battles during the remainder of the war. Because of this incident with Callaway County *vs.* the United States of America, locals began to call the place "The Kingdom of Callaway." You still see signs of this in many places.   Remember the earlier story about Kingdom City?

I'll come back to talk about reasons to visit Fulton today but I must mention just a few of the notable people who have called Fulton home. Do you remember "the Callaway Kid?" Bake McBride was a Cardinal standout and Rookie of the Year. Tony Galbreath was a great one for Mizzou and then played for years in the NFL.

Helen Stevens was known worldwide as "The Fulton Flash." She was the fastest woman in the world and made a shambles of Hitler's Berlin Olympic hopes.   He came to congratulate her for her success and tried to hug her but she said "I just gave him a good old Missouri handshake." You can read more about her in *Tales from Missouri and the Heartland.*

Fulton resident, Henry Bellamann wrote a novel, King's Row, which some feel was based on his home town. It was later made into a movie starring Ann Sheridan, Robert Cummings, Ronald Reagan, and Betty Field.

Fulton has been the home to higher education since 1842. The campuses of William Woods University and Westminster College are beautiful sections of the town. In 1946 Sir Winston Churchill announced that he would come to Fulton to deliver a major speech. With the world's press corps looking on he declared that an Iron Curtain had descended across

Europe. This speech warned the world that the Cold War was on and it was a serious matter.

Because of the historical significance of that speech, a number of world leaders have come to make speeches annually ever since. Some of the speakers have been <u>Lech Wałęsa</u>, <u>Margaret Thatcher</u>, <u>Harry Truman</u>, <u>Gerald Ford</u>, <u>Ronald Reagan</u>, <u>George H. W. Bush</u>, <u>Mikhail Gorbachev</u> and <u>NATO</u> representatives.

Westminster has a special chapel on campus which originally sat in the heart of London. It was designed by Sir Christopher Wren. In 1969 it was shipped to Fulton and re-assembled. After the fall of the Berlin Wall Churchill's granddaughter arranged for a section of the wall to be sent to the campus and erected as an imposing sculpture near the Wren church. In the church's lower level is a very fine museum that every Missourian should plan to visit.

Berlin Wall Sculpture

And there is still a lot more to see and do in Fulton. Have you been to the Kemper Center for the Arts? It is surrounded by a sculpture garden which is worth the trip all by itself. A totally different kind of museum is the Backer Auto World Museum. The museum organization actually owns many more cars but eighty of them are to be seen at any one time in the newly remodeled facility. The facility itself is a surprisingly nice venue. In addition to vintage cars, Auto World contains exhibits and collections of memorabilia and attractions depicting the history of the automobile, in Missouri.

Plan your trip accordingly because at some time during your visit you will want to stop in at the Soda Fountain in Sault's Drug Store. You can relax in the old fashioned setting with a cup of coffee or enjoy a cold treat made with Central Dairy ice cream. The fountain serves a variety of milkshakes, malts, smoothies, floats, phosphates, banana splits, sundaes, ice cream sodas, and much more!

*(**Hint**) This writer has found that grandchildren will always be on their best behavior if they know that a Central Dairy reward is waiting for them. I suspect that even my wife treats me better when Central Dairy ice cream is on the agenda.*

Overland

Back in the early 1820s St. Louis was definitely the Gateway to the West. Wagon trains traveled on the Overland Trail from that city to points beyond. For most, the first stop west of St. Louis was just twelve miles away. It was a park-like area known as Overland Park and it had an open field and a good dependable spring. As time went by, an inn was built here and named Twelve Mile Inn. When a town sprung up at the location, it was named Overland because of its place on that Overland Trail.

Markers have been placed at these historic places. Other historic places in Overland include the Dennis Lackland House and the nearby McElhinney Log House, built in the 1850s. The Ritenour School was built in 1867 and , believe it or not, it is still in use. It is now the school district's administration building.

If you visit Overland, I hope that it might be in December when the lights are all on at Dan's Emerald Forest. Whether or not you see the lights, you will want to see this elaborate outdoor train display. Dan Schmidt is a professional landscaper who has arranged his model railroads to run through his front yard, across the front porch, into and back out of his house, and past all sorts of scenery. It's a unique and special place provided by one of those people who give of themselves to make our world more interesting.

Patton

. Some say that there were descendants of the members of the James Gang still living in Bollinger County as recently as the 1930s. That just might be so. You'll certainly wonder if you step out into the cemetery at the United Methodist Church on County Road 878 near Patton.   There you will find a monument to a killing.

Edward Capehart O'Kelley was born and raised in Patton. In 1858 he shot and killed Robert Ford. You may remember that Robert Ford was "that dirty little coward, that shot Mr. Howard, and lowered Jesse James in his grave." That revenge killing is memorialized in the church cemetery.

While you might like to see that, the real reason for visiting Patton is on the property of Steve and Alice Wagoner. They call it "The Circle" but it is a set of twelve stones placed according to the position of the sun at the summer solstice and they form a henge. The stones are as large as seven tons and they really do resemble England's Stonehenge. Of course they're smaller but impressive just the same. It's just a little west of Cape Girardeau and Jackson and you really should see them if possible.

There's something else about Patton that we can't see but I wish we could. It was "a tale of two kitties." The Marquand Tigers ran into some bad luck when they played the Patton Panthers basketball team on February 10, 2006. The boys' basketball team from Patton set a national record for the number of three-pointers (36) in a single high school basketball game. That's 108 points without even counting the two-pointers and free throws!

It's the Little Things. . .

We had a section earlier in this book about gigantic things. There are also some interesting small things in the state. For Instance, at Mt. Vernon there is a very tiny church. **Shepherd's Field Wedding Chapel** is said to be the Smallest Chapel in use in the state of Missouri. Some will tell you that it's the smallest in the United States. The Chapel is 6'x10' outside dimensions and can hold a wedding party of 10. I think it was really intended to be used as a backdrop for outside weddings. It's on Farm Road 2137 so you will need a good map or you can google the directions.

There is a smaller and better **church** between Hannibal and Bowling Green near **Frankford**. This little white frame building has windows and everything. Follow Route C out of Frankford for about five miles.

OK, that one is kind of silly. I admit it but this one is much better. At Long Lane there sits a building which was for years, a genuine working bank. **The First State Bank of Long Lane** was incorporated in 1910 and was an important part of the little community. It even survived the Great Depression and a robbery in the 1930s. It couldn't survive the automobile however and locals began to drive to bigger institutions in Buffalo. At about 12 feet by 20 feet, it really is tiny and, if you happen to be driving down Highway 32, watch for it.

It's the Little Things (cont.). . .

Glencoe, Missouri has something as great as it is tiny. The **Wabash, Frisco, and Pacific Railroad** operates a little 12 inch gauge railroad that runs with actual steam engines. The WF&P RR was organized in 1939 and these railroad enthusiasts build the little trains and the tracks, roundhouses, water towers, and everything else needed to take you on a trip through the Ozarks countryside. They do charge $4.00 but it's worth it. Kids, parents, and grandparents of all ages show up for this and enjoy it.

You can hop aboard the WF&P RR on Sunday afternoons from May through October. Please remember, this is not a commercial operation. It's just a bunch of nice people wanting to have fun.

Florissant

It's easy to forget about Florissant as we fight the traffic of an urban Interstate beltway. There are so many things to compete for our attention. However, if you will slow down to pay attention, there are some jewels there for you. Entire books have been written about the history of this place and some historians say that the original settlement was as old as St. Louis. Spanish records in Havana, Cuba show that in 1787 there were already forty people and seven plantations operating in Florissant. In 1793 five residents were killed in an Indian attack but the settlement continued.

The French called this place "Fleurissant," or "Blooming" while the Spanish called it "St. Ferdinand." Today residents call it "The Valley of Flowers." We can still see some of the Spanish and much of the French influence. There are literally dozens of well-preserved historic buildings dating back to the 1700s. The **Auguste Aubuchon House at** 1002 rue St. Louis is over two centuries old.

John B. Myers House at 180 Dunn Road is a farm with buildings almost 150 years old. It is a "working complex" occupied by yarn and fabric shops with a barn deli. The **Magill House** at 410 Harrison is an example of what the town calls the white brick period. The original portion of house built about 1830. The Spanish Land Grant Park at St. Denis and St. Ferdinand was a gift of the Spanish King to the inhabitants of the village of St. Ferdinand. Once the Place d'Arms where the militia drilled. Many of the early settlers lie here in unmarked graves.

Tower Court Log Cabin in Tower Court Park, Washington and New Florissant Road, was probably built by a trapper around 1850, the cabin is still located on its original site. **Taille de Noyer** is located on campus of McCluer High School. Once an Indian trading post, later the hunting lodge of John Mullanphy, one of Missouri's most illustrious citizens, it became the country home of Mullanphy's descendants, then the Florissant Valley Historical Society restored it as a house museum.

To this writer, the Old St. Ferdinand Shrine is at # 1 rue St. Francois is the most significant of the dozens of ancient buildings. Old St. Ferdinand Shrine is the oldest Catholic Church building in the Louisiana Purchase Territory. The convent wing was built in 1819 for Mother Rose Philippine

Duchesne and 3 other Sacred Heart Nuns. The corner stone of the current church was laid in 1821 by Mother Duchesne. In 1988 the pioneering Mother Duchesne was declared a Saint by the Catholic Church. Old St. Ferdinand was elevated to Shrine status. Father DeSmet, the beloved "Black Robe" of the Indian nations, was ordained here on September 23, 1827. This is not still an active church so please be sure to contact the shrine before you go.

Mills Across Missouri

There are literally hundreds of old mills rotting away across the state. At one time their water powered equipment was an essential part of frontier life. In season the mills operated 24 hours a day every day except Sundays but the farmers might still have to wait for a day or two or more to get their grain ground. So the mills became a place where other commerce might spring up such as a general store, a blacksmith shop, or anything else needed to serve the local needs. In seasons when the grindstones of the grist mill were not needed, the mill could be converted to a lumber mill. They were certainly places where people could discuss religion, politics, and local news.

Before rural electrification mills could easily be rigged to run a generator so a mill might be the only place that some folks would ever see electricity in use. These high tech. businesses were everywhere where the state's rivers and streams would allow and that included every county in Missouri. So even though what remains of some mills can still be seen in many places around us, I have chosen to mention only the very best of the bunch – the ones that show us a little of our ancestor's lives.

As I prepared this book for publication I was amazed at the number of old water mills that still exist. In fact there are two of them that I drive by routinely and didn't even recognize them for what they are. They now appear to be very large old warehouse or factory buildings and, in many cases, that's what they have become. But in their glory days they were the center of community life and the very reason for towns to spring up where they did. In some towns the brick ones have been converted into modern offices in charming old buildings.

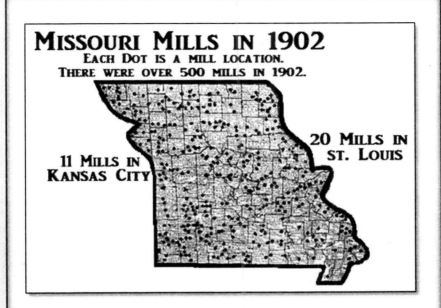

MISSOURI MILLS IN 1902
EACH DOT IS A MILL LOCATION.
THERE WERE OVER 500 MILLS IN 1902.

20 MILLS IN ST. LOUIS

11 MILLS IN KANSAS CITY

We also want to remember that many mills were not water-powered but had steam engines. These were often replaced by internal combustion engines or even diesel engines in their later years. Here are some good ones that still look like and sometimes even serve as grist mills.

Way down in Ozark County there are five historic mills. On the North Fork of the White River sits the **Dawt Mill**. Huge, rustic, wonderful and lots to do. It's on a back road a couple of miles from the junction of Highways 160 and PP east of Gainesville. Just upstream from Tecumseh. About 15 miles northwest of Gainesville is the **Hammond Mill**. This big stone and wood frame structure really needs someone to love it. It's too good to be lost to wood rot or termites.

At the south edge of the Mark Twain National Forest and east of Sycamore The **Rockbridge Mill** sits on the North Fork of the White. It is easy to reach by following the signs on Highway N. This big barn-red structure sits on the edge of an extra nice pebble beach. You will want to have a meal in the Rockbridge General Store and Restaurant. It's known for the fresh rainbow trout and for wonderful cobblers.

Zanoni Mill is very close to the Rockbridge Mill but visible from the highway. Sadly, it's not open to the public. Zanoni is also a very large wood frame building but it is painted white with a huge "overshot" water wheel and a pleasant mill pond.

Hodgson Mill is the jewel of the Ozarks that you see pictured on so many calendars and posters. It's a wonderful red structure built to take advantage of the Bryant Creek's spring that gushes three million gallons of 58° water daily. Add in a cave, a fern grotto, and the beautiful scenery – This is a wonderful place! It's easy to find too from Highway 181.

Next door in Shannon County you will find **Alley Spring Mill**. This beautiful spot has a great three-story red mill built at the site of a natural spring. It's also the site (about 100 yards away) of a nice one-room schoolhouse. There is a great history here that well-represents the place of mills as the center of frontier community life. It's open every day in summer months and it's free but donations are expected.

How about a tiny little log and stone mill with a huge water wheel and a moss covered shake roof? Sound picturesque doesn't it? It's **Reed Spring Mill** near Centerville and just off Highway 21. This little building sits on the Black River.

Just a few miles east in Oregon County is an unusual small mill named for its power source. **Falling Spring Mill** is owned by the state park system and is worth a stop because of its setting. Just south of the Oregon-Shannon County line look for a very small brown sign that says just, "Falling Spring." The name indicates its water fall.

If you're in Southeast Missouri, you must stop at the **Bollinger Mill**. It's easy to find just south of Jackson. Take Highway 34 to County Road HH and watch for the signs. You will find a three-story stone and brick mill with a good dam, a mill pond, and even a covered bridge! This is a state owned historic site and has lots of history (back to 1797) for those who are interested.

Up in Crawford County you can visit the **Dillard Mill**. While this one is not as picturesque as Bollinger, it is still a very pretty red building beside the beautiful fresh Huzzah River. The great part about this one is what you find inside. The original equipment is still there, massive, innovative, primitive, and impressive. It's wonderful stuff! Dillard Mill is pictured on the front cover of this book.

Topaz Mill is south of Cabool and west of Willow Springs. Until 1930 it was powered by the North Fork of the White River. Its beautifully clear mill pond is fed by the Topaz Spring and the barn red three-story structure is sided by a two-story water wheel. Today it is privately owned and the owners are the ones who have wonderfully restored and preserved the property. Their rights must be respected but they do allow visitors. From the intersection of Highways 76 and 181, go south on County Road E.

In Lawson, MO the **Watkins Woolen Mill** State Park is not like the picturesque mills of the Ozarks but it is a very significant place. It's a great museum with the original equipment in place and very much worth your visit.

Montauk Mill is about 20 miles southwest of Salem on Highway 19. Several springs in the park combine with tiny Pigeon Creek to supply 43 million gallons of water to the river each day. This forms the headers of the Current River which powers the mill. The state's parks department runs this and it's a good place to see what mills were like over a century ago.

Edwards Mill is something totally different from all the rest. It's right in the middle of the campus of College of the Ozarks in Point Lookout, five miles south of Branson. It was built using timber harvested from older Missouri mills and it is an outstanding example of the early 1900s milling process. This is actually a working grist mill and students from the college operate it.

Using a 12 foot water wheel, the students grind whole-grain flour and you can actually buy some right there at the mill. The basement is sort of a milling museum and the upstairs is a weaving studio where you can buy what the students make. Remember, these students don't pay tuition. Instead they do work like this to pay for their higher education. It's a special place and you can help them while you're enjoying yourself. Everybody wins!

September brings an opportunity to visit the big three-story Licking Mill. The town showcases artists, crafters, and musicians in the mill.

A Final Thought –

Several of these wonderful structures have been restored and preserved by some family's hard work and a small fortune. We owe them a great deal of appreciation and when visiting their places, we want to be sure and respect their wishes. Otherwise we will begin to find more private roads gated and locked.

NOTE: As this Second Edition is being prepared, an old mill is also being prepared for its new life as a bistro. **The Gerald Mill,** *right on U.S. Highway 50 in Gerald, MO, is being remodeled by descendants of an earlier owner. These experienced restaurateurs from the Branson and Springfield areas are preserving the massive oak beams and the cast iron gears overhead as ambience to go along with their gourmet sandwiches and Missouri wines. There will also be local entertainers performing from time to time.*

*I plan to visit the **Gerald Mill** soon. Maybe I'll see you there!*

Clarksville

Clarksville's motto is "Unhurried, Unspoiled, Uncommon." That's really pretty good because it fits. This pretty little town sits right on the Great River Road and looks out on the Mighty Mississippi. In the winter you can find a comfortable viewing spot and watch the bald eagles go about their work of fishing the Mississippi. This is, after all, one of the best places in the lower forty eight for bald eagles to gather when their fishing areas freeze farther north.

In the warmer weather the eagles aren't as plentiful but there is much more to do. For one thing, you can take the sky lift to the top of Lookout Point Hill. From there you can see the river valley for 800 square miles around you. This pleasant town has come to be the permanent home for a variety of artists including painters, potters, jewelry and glass makers, and specialty craftsmen.

This community actually dates back to a settlement in the first decade of the 1800s but that settlement was wiped out by Indians. The settlers were back in 1817 and that is when they first called themselves Clarksville, in honor of the famous explorer and Governor, William Clark. By 1820 the very first steamboat north of St. Louis pulled into Clarksville and left with a huge quantity of tobacco bound for Europe and elsewhere.

By 1860 Clarksville had grown to a population of almost 1200 people and it contained mills, factories, markets, and shops of all kinds. Local vineyards were producing 12,000 gallons of wine per year. The railroad came through in 1870 and is still an important part of the town today. With the coming of the railroad, the population grew by another 25%. Today however, the population is less than 500. The net effect is that this picturesque river town had a steady prosperity which produced some fine buildings but, when growth stopped, the old buildings were spared and not lost to progress. This is why people today still drive to spend their days in this nice time capsule.

I want to make special note of the Windsor Chair Shop right there on First Street. Caron and Ralph Quick are famous nationally for the chairs they make using the materials and techniques of the 1700s. These nice people make wonderful products and their shop is open to visitors. This is a unique workshop and worth your attention.

Ilasco

Ilasco is not a city. It's not even a town. But after the first edition of this book was published, a surprising number of people looked at the contents searching for Ilasco. Others suggested that it be in the next edition. Now I understand why.

In 1901 the Atlas Portland Cement Company made the decision to begin operations near Hannibal and they purchased 1144 acres of land. There they built barracks and began to entice a labor force. African-Americans arrived from South Carolina and many more workers were attracted to the place from Poland, Romania, Hungary and other Slavic countries. They named the now town Ilasco representing the essential elements needed for making cement - iron, lime, alumina, silica, coal and oxygen.

A common practice of that time was for the company to build "company towns" with their own rented housing and "company stores." Leaders in Hannibal pressured Atlas to prevent that from happening and a railroad was built for the workers to take them home each night to Hannibal. They did most of their shopping in Hannibal but there were a limited amount of privately-owned stores and a few houses in Ilasco itself.

This first cement plant west of the Mississippi was quickly turning out cement for the Keokuk Dam, the Panama Canal, and the Empire State Building along with many other well-known places. The Panama Canal alone use over four million barrels of this Missouri cement.

The little town grew and more and more immigrants arrived and soon it even had its own little suburb. The name of the suburb was Monkey Run but no one knows just why. The immigrants, were usually young, hard-working, and well educated. Many of them spoke several languages. Eventually these immigrants to the little Ilasco community became full-fledged citizens in Hannibal and added a great deal to the life of that city.

This little town that never quite became a town was the magnet that drew thousands of new Americans to Missouri. For the purposes of this book – well, it's like they say in the detective shows, "Just keep on moving, folks. There's nothing to see here." But even if there is nothing for us to see in Ilasco, there is a good deal for us to know about and be aware. Ilasco's story is the story of America growing up.

MORE Food Challenges

Remember to call ahead before you go. These contests change quickly.

Cape Girardeau has an offer of $100.00 if you can eat El Durango. It's a six pound burrito. A short distance away you'll find the Pizzaria Adagio where they serve something called the Symphony Pizza. It's only 14 inches wide but it's a monster just the same. It's yours along with your name on the Wall of Fame if you can down it in just one hour.

The Essential Kneads Dayspa and Café in **Chillicothe** serves a burger they call The Flamer. It's a spicy burger. It's a very spicy burger and eating it plus one tater tot afterwards will earn you a coupon for another burger.

I want to hang around **Dexter** and watch the people take the challenges there. It's Man vs. Fish at Fiddler's Fish House. This challenge has twenty fish filets, baked beans, slaw, potato wedges and eight hush puppies. Or, over at Rulo's Smoked Barbeque place, you can try the Colossus. It's a big 4 ½ pound burger stuffed with a pound of pulled pork. It comes with a pound of brisket, a pint of macaroni and cheese and a pint of baked beans. Speaking of "stuffed with!" It's free if you polish it off in just one hour.

Food Challenges (cont.)

Spokes Pub & Grill at **Farmington** has a very unique challenge. They offer the meal free to anyone who can eat their three "hamburgers." One is made with beef, one with buffalo, and the other is elk. And, yes, it has been done.

The Bar 12 Sports Grill in **Kansas City** offers a five pound plate of nachos called Monster Nachos for free if you can finish them in less than an hour. One person finished in only 22 minutes.

What's in a 3½ pound Reuben sandwich? At Governor Stumpy's Grill House in **Kansas City**, that would be one pound of corned beef, ½ pound of sauerkraut, six pieces of rye bread, and six slices of melted Swiss cheese. That, along with one pound of French fries, makes The Reubenator challenge. Eat that in less than an hour and you get a free tee shirt. Cholesterol tests are extra.

Food Challenges (cont.)

Still in **Kansas City**, I'm sure you will want to visit Jess & Jim's. They offer a 75 ounce steak for free if you can eat it all. Now I have to admit that there are more than a dozen other noteworthy food challenges in K.C. and I have only listed some of the most intriguing. I also want to give a special notice to two place names. My vote for the best name at an eatery is Governor Stumpy's Grill House. My vote for the most suggestive name would go to the Scoop &Scoot Deli.

Little **Rockport**, MO offers a 77 oz. steak for free if you can eat it in less than an hour. This is at the Black Iron Grill. Philly's Pizza in **Marthasville** will give you fifty wings free if you can eat them in less than an hour.

Now we're getting ridiculous: Dublin's Pass in **Springfield** offers the Dublin Dare. It's a sandwich with four smash patties, corned beef, rashers, and bangers, all on a Kaiser bun. It comes with a pound of fries, a quart of beer and a Dublin Drop Shot. You get it free and a tee shirt also if you will just clean your plate in 30 minutes or less.

Food Challenges (cont.)

And really ridiculous: Eros on Main in **St. Charles** invites you to dine on their Trojan Horse Sandwich. It's a big one and it costs $29.95 but you can get it free if you'll just eat it. The problem is that the sandwich itself weighs ten pounds and it comes with a required two pounds of French fries.

Finally, if I were to try one of these I would go for the one at T's Redneck Steakhouse in **Lebanon**. That's partly because I enjoy their good food often. They challenge you to finish their five pound pork chop that comes along with a sweet potato, a salad, and a dinner roll. If you can do so in less than one hour, you get the meal free and you get a tee shirt so you can prove that you did it.

Yes, people do win this challenge from time to time. About the only catch is that you have to give them 24 hours notice so they can get the special cut of meat.

Bon Appetite!

Knob Noster

Outstate Missourians often refer to round-topped hills as knobs. You may remember that the vigilante group down on the Arkansas border liked to meet on bald knobs (having no trees). That way they could see trouble coming from a distance. So they were called Bald Knobbers. Well, up here in the middle of the state there are knobs also. Between Kansas City and Sedalia there are two very noticeable knobs right by Highway 50. The locals referred to them as "Our Knobs" and the Latin term for "our" is "noster." Put it all together and you get Knob Noster.

Let's, for a minute, go back to December 7, 1941 at Pearl Harbor, Hawaii. There was a young pilot there named George Whiteman. George was born at Longwood, MO and graduated from high school at Sedalia and then from college at UM-Rolla. Then, after training he was sent for duty in Hawaii. On that morning of infamy he scrambled to his fighter plane and had just lifted off when a Japanese Zero caught him from behind and shot him down. He crashed at the end of the runway and became the first American pilot killed in World War II. It was this George Whiteman for whom the Whiteman Air Force Base at Knob Noster is named.

2nd Lt. George Whiteman

In just a little time you can learn a lot and see all sorts of interesting things at Whiteman. For one thing, our entire fleet of stealth bombers calls Whiteman home. That's right, every time a mission is flown to any place in the world, the bombers take off from Knob Noster and return there when the job is done. And yes, you can see the fantastic futuristic looking craft at the base. If you're lucky you will see them take off and/or land.

Oscar One is another interesting thing to see. During the Cold War, our countryside was dotted with 2,200 Inter-Continental Ballistic Missiles. The launch command post for many of those was at Whiteman in a building called Oscar One. Today it's just a piece of history but it is on the base tour so you can walk through and maybe sit in the command chair. Don't worry, when you push that button, nothing happens.

Today Knob Noster prospers because of its agriculture, its nearby Knob Noster State Park, and the Whiteman A.F.B. Go ahead. Get off the interstate and check this place out.

De Soto

.The basic impression one gets arriving in De Soto is that of the beautiful tree-covered hills. That is exactly what greeted the first settler, Isaac Van Metre, when he arrived over two hundred years ago. Then he found water and lots of it. The Joachim Creek runs through the valley and several springs feed into the creek from this very spot. Because of this, he built a cabin here in 1803. With plenty of wild game and bottom land he could provide well for his family. Today's visitor to De Soto can see an obelisk marking the spot where Van Metre built his home. And, by the way, these springs and wells gave the town its nickname of "Fountain City."

In 1851 the Iron Mountain Railroad announced plans to build from the Iron Mines to the river port in St. Louis. This started a great deal of speculation and growth in De Soto. An important boost for the town came when the two-story depot, roundhouse, and locomotive shop were built. This made De Soto an important railroad town and shaped the very appearance of the place right up to today.

The early 1900s were significant for many reasons. In 1915 the town removed the large stones that spanned the major streets from curb to curb. Of course the roadways were dirt or mud depending on the weather. And the horses added elements of their own. So these stones served the purpose of stepping stones to keep clothing and shoes clean and dry. The problem was that automobiles began to arrive in town and they couldn't handle the large stones across the streets.

The town also had three bridges across the creek. One was for wagons, another was a swinging bridge, and another, called the wire bridge was like an earlier, smaller version of the Golden Gate Bridge. Now we put up culverts and pay little attention to streams.

In 1931 Mel Bay graduated from De Soto High School and went on to revolutionize the playing and teaching of string and wind instruments. I wonder how many people who read this book have also used Mel Bay's music books and studied the "Mel Bay Method."

Older readers will also remember the days when we mailed our camera film away to be developed and a few days later the pictures would come back to us in the mail. If you did that, you probably sent your film to Fo-Jo Studios. And, yes, those studios were right here in De Soto.

Possibly the main reason for tourists to visit De Soto today is to see what the Mississippian Indians left for us 3000 years ago. In nearby Washington State Park you will see mysterious petroglyphs carved into the rocks. In their book, *Indians and Archaeology of Missouri,* Carl and Eleanor Chapman tell us that this was, "probably the junction of game trails and war trails, and was possibly a consecrated spot where young men were initiated into secret society rites and were taught the mythology associated with the initiation." It was a special place thousands of years ago and, because of that, it is today also.

Some places make impressions on you and make you think of different things. When I look at De Soto today my mind pictures this place and others from a hundred or so years ago. I see a mental movie of a railroad town with lots of bustle, a big hotel, and a parade of interesting people waiting to act out some of life's dramas. And I'll bet that my imaginings are not too far from reality.

Excelsior Springs

What an interesting place this is! In fact, if I headed a large business that needed a new headquarters location, the first place I would check out is Excelsior Springs. The hilly curvy streets lead to a downtown that is picturesque, historic, spacious, and just hungering for a renaissance. Of course it's also close to Kansas City, an international airport, and the interstate highway system.

I'll admit that it's sad to see this special place so quiet but I'm also suggesting that you use that to your advantage. The parking is free and plentiful and there are almost never crowds to contend with. You can see the sights truly at you leisure.

In 1880 settlers discovered a mineral spring and thought it to have medicinal qualities. Eventually 20 springs bubbling out four distinct varieties were discovered and tapped. So that same year Excelsior Springs was founded. As time went by the mineral waters were bottled and sold across the nation and the world. But, if these waters are good to drink, wouldn't they also be good for bathing? Soon spas were opening with the most famous of them the National Register Elms Hotel, built 1912. President Harry Truman spent the 1948 election night at the Elms. Remember the next morning when he held up that newspaper saying that Dewey was the new President. That happened at the Elms.

The Elms Hotel & Spa!

In 1935 the Hall of Waters was built and it features the world's longest water bar as well as exhibits about the history of the city in its beautiful solarium. The building also houses the city government offices. We can't forget that Rev. Robert Sallee James owned a farm near Excelsior Springs. He was a prominent farmer and minister. He founded two churches which still exist today and was a co-founder of nearby William Jewell College. Of course his sons, Frank and Jesse, became sort of famous also.

The Downtown Villas Project offers hope to this city. It will create 31 brand new homes and everyone expects it to spur growth in this place that deserves a shot in the arm. Let's just hope that this quiet friendly town with the unique history will remember and preserve its heritage as it grows into the future.

St. Charles

No one is going to say that St. Charles is out of the way or off the beaten path. It's one of the oldest, best known, most populace, and busiest communities in our state. However, it seems to me that many people go to the Bass Pro Shop and then get right back on Interstate 70. If you're one of those folks, you are missing a great deal.

Entire books have been written about the history of this town but I'll mention just a few of the folks who have been here before you. Think of Lewis and Clark, Sacajawea, Daniel Boone and his family and friends, George and Mary Sibley, our earliest lawmakers, mountain men, pioneers, military leaders, and adventurers. They were all here when the Missouri River was the only route to the west and all of them have left their mark on this unique place.

I suggest that you stop at any of the tourist information centers and pick up a map or guide book. Then it's an easy matter to navigate the little brick or cobblestone streets to the places you will like the most. If you happen to be here in

December, the old part of town is even more charming than usual.

You'll have to pick and choose when it comes to doing things in St. Charles but I'll point out a few. You really should stop on First Capital Drive and see our state's first capitol building. Maybe you will want to visit the Foundry Art Center, or the Haviland Museum, or the Frenchtown Heritage Museum.

Maybe you will want to ride the Golden Eagle Ferry across the wide Missouri. Kids love this! Speaking of boats, how about visiting the Boat House and Nature Center. Here you can see exact replicas of Lewis and Clark's river craft. The Missouri Wing of the Commemorative Air Force is housed at Smartt Airport and it has three World War II aircraft for you to see. And of course, the riverfront is dominated by one of the immediate area's casinos. Whatever you choose to do in St. Charles, one thing is certain – you can't really enjoy this place from behind the wheel of your car. You must have your feet on the cobblestones and give yourself time to enjoy it all.

At the corner of South Main and Boonslick Road you can find an unusually good restaurant with its own micro-brewery. The Trailhead Brewing Company features a good family menu that also pleases the young up-and-comers crowd including those young people who have passed middle age. In other words, they have something to please everyone. They also serve some very distinctive beers and each is worth trying. You won't be disappointed with any of them!

Here's an idea for you. Ask your Trailhead server to bring several glasses with your order. Then, each adult can order a different beer, and you can pass them around and do some sampling.

Bob's Gasoline Alley

I know. You always meant to stop there. Well, maybe
first you should know about Bob. Bob is a collector and he
collects whatever strikes his fancy. The result is that a visit to
his place keeps you guessing about what you might see next.
Even driving past on I-44 keeps you guessing. You can always
count on his antique gas station pole signs. You even see them
at night because they're all lit up. What you never know is who
will be grazing in his fields.

This writer has seen emus, ostriches, longhorn cattle,
llamas, alpacas, miniature horses, donkeys, burros, guinea fowl,
turkeys, fallow deer, barnyard pets, and more. Bob also has
antique clocks, gas pumps, signs, anything to do with old Route
66. And they all light up and work to perfection! Some days
he hosts antique auto shows, and meetings for people who love
Route 66.

So is this a museum? Not exactly. It's Bob's home and
he just happens to have collected some wonderful old stuff. It's
not really open to the public but Bob can usually be available to

~ 259 ~

show his collection to anyone with a genuine interest. If you haven't realized it yet, Bob's Gasoline Alley is a strip of land bordered by Interstate 44 on one side and the old Route 66 on the other. It's located between Cuba and St. James near exit 203. If you are serious about seeing his collection, you must call Bob in advance and make an appointment. His number is (573) 885-3637.

Ste. Genevieve

Ste. Genevieve is known by every schoolchild to be the oldest permanent European settlement in Missouri. But it's my experience that people on the western side of the state don't understand just what this little city has done to save our heritage and just what interesting experiences are there for us. Originally settled by French and then surrounded by German settlers, the results are still obvious. In addition to the names on the streets and businesses, you can see the vineyards and wineries. The historic district has very old cabins that are very different from any other cabins in the state.

You see the French did not stack the logs for their buildings horizontally as other folks did. Instead, they dug a trench and placed their logs sticking up vertically from the ground. This gives the building a very different look. Then they covered the roofs with thatch. Latter the thatch was replaced with wooden shingles and that is what you see today. They also invented a way to cope with our summer heat by surrounding the entire houses with big porches (galleries). Besides giving the houses a distinctive look, this would allow the residents to always be in the shade or the sun depending on the weather and the breezes.

Since they were right on the river, fine furniture could be brought right to them by boat. So these homes looked fairly primitive on the outside but were often furnished beautifully. The learned that grass was a good hiding place for rodents and snakes so these early settlers had no grass in their "yards." But they had very attractive gardens. What I'm trying to point out is that these homes were very different from what most people expect and the tours are extremely interesting.

The great fire of 1849 destroyed the old French section of St. Louis and other French settlements just weren't as aware of their heritage as the residents of Ste. Genevieve. We owe these individuals our genuine thanks and praise for preserving what they have. In fact, they have saved the largest collection of French-Colonial buildings in all of North America.

Ste. Gen also has lots of brick buildings. In fact the oldest brick house west of the Mississippi still stands at Third and Market. While it just looks old and plain on the outside, the inside holds a very attractive restaurant serving very good meals. Today's visitor will find several places for fine dining in the downtown area alone.

The Big Field Restaurant is the place for authentic Cajun fare. If you love Cajun, you must stop here. For light meals and coffee, the Station No. 2 restaurant is located in an old fire station. Food is good, prices are low, and kids will thank you for this. The Anvil is located in a very old saloon. Its prices are a little higher but everyone loves this place.

I suggest that you begin your Ste. Genevieve experience at the Great River Road Interpretive Center. It is also the Tourist Information Office located at the corner of Market and Main Streets. They are helpful and knowledgeable and they can give you a nice little map so you won't miss anything important.

Before you leave town you owe it to yourself to make two purchases. First, the local vintners produce many varieties of either French- or German-style wines. Ask the retailer for suggestions. The second stop should be at Oberle Meats. This modern shop has a long tradition. For over 140 years the Oberle family has been making what they called German bologna but what the rest of us call Oberle Sausage. It's right on Highway 32 and the meats and cheeses are worth the stop.

Defiance

Defiance is a destination point for many. It's an interesting little place to drive through for others. Others cycle through on the Katy Trail. Highway 94 is an old road that connects Jefferson City with St. Charles. It passes near Washington and through Defiance, Augusta, and the Busch Wildlife Area on its way between Jeff City and St. Charles and then it goes on eastward to the Alton Bridge at the Mississippi.

It can be intimidating to drive into town and be greeted with the sight of fifty or sixty big motorcycles gathered around one of the taverns. However, since this writer has lived nearby for over a quarter century, I have heard of no problems with these bikers. They are not the Hell's Angels. They are instead some nice folks who like to ride and the like to find places to congregate with other similar riders. In this way they are very similar to the bikers I mentioned earlier at Devil's Elbow.

It seems that Defiance has been a meeting place since before recorded history. The Osage, Missouri, and other Indian nations have left traces of their meetings going way back to the

Mississippians. Over two centuries ago Daniel Boone sat under a tree at this place and served as a judge in local disputes. The Judgment Tree is gone now but a marker at its location still stands down by the river.

Ol' Dan'l is probably the main reason that people come to this place. His home is just north of town but you have to travel east from Defiance and get on Highway F to reach the place. Some people love to argue that this beautiful stone residence is actually Nathan Boone's home and it is true that Nathan and his family lived here. But Daniel lived here and Daniel was the head of the family. This is where everyone came to meet the great explorer.

For many years this home was owned and preserved by Boone descendants and they did it with love. I must admit that I enjoyed visiting here more when the family was in charge. But as time went by, the task became more overwhelming and increasingly expensive. So the Boone descendants turned the property over to Lindenwood University. Giving credit where it is due, the staff and students at Lindenwood have done some wonderful things with the property.

The side of the home which people recognize as the front was really the rear and the true "front" of the place was the side with the porches overlooking the valley. In this valley the folks from Lindenwood have created something they call

Boonesfield Village. This village is a collection of historic buildings gathered from the area and preserved here for you to see. In some cases the buildings would have been lost altogether if not for Lindenwood.

This little village has the home of the famous Sappington family, and many businesses plus a church and a school from the late 1700s to the early 1800s. It's a wonderful place staffed by university students and local amateur historians. Now here is something different – I urge you to visit this place at least twice for two completely different experiences.

First, visit on some warm day and walk the grounds when the doors are open and the logs and stones do their own natural insulating. You will get a feel for what the pioneers experienced. Sit in on a lesson at the school. Talk with the blacksmith, and the grocer. Listen to the fantastic pump organ in the church. Watch the craftsmen and women making baskets, candles, soap, and more. Usually you can even talk with "Daniel."

Second, visit on a dark December evening. The entire village and its pathways are framed by thousands of candles in luminaries. Acoustic instruments strum carols and singers serenade you as you stroll or stand near a warm fire. The homes and shops are open and everything is lighted by candles and fireplaces just as in the old days. You will never forget this experience!

When you visit the Sappington-Drexel House you can sip some warm wassail and sing carols accompanied by a harpsichord. (♫Here we go a-wassailing♫) You will be amazed at how bright the home is when lighted only by candles in chandeliers.

For this December visit, overdress. Wear more layers of clothing than you would expect to be necessary. We are not as tough as our predecessors and we need to be prepared. You can always un-button a little or take off one layer but I'll bet you won't. Take your best gloves and warmest hat because to really experience this, you will need to be outside for a long time.

This little trip, especially when taken with children, will be greatly enhanced if you will study a little in advance about the lives of Daniel and his son, Nathan Boone. Both were extremely important in the growth of this state and both were flawed humans who still managed to become admirable and heroic. And don't forget about the Boones in this book's sections on Ash Grove and Dutzow.

<u>Vintage Base Ball</u>

(St. Louis)

Picture this: The arbiter calls, "Striker to the line." The hurler stands in the middle of the diamond with his feet crossed. Then, when the striker is ready, the hurler steps forward, and tosses. A mighty swing but the striker has missed. The ball bounces to the behind. The behind throws it back to the hurler for another try. Once more the hurler tosses a dew drop to Tree Knocker who strikes a mighty blow. The ball flies through the air toward the garden but the scout has been playing deep and he runs forward to catch the missile barehanded on one bound. "The striker is dead!" the arbiter roars and the scorer records the event on the <u>Griesedieck Brothers scoreboard</u>.

The Cranks have been quiet until now but they roar their approval. "Well hit, sir!" and "Well played!" comes from both sides of the field. "Bully!" "Huzzah!" The spectators appreciate the effort of the player no matter whether he is for the Perfectos or the Unions. Cheering for a good play is and always has been part of "the St. Louis way" and the admiration means that the center fielder's jammed fingers won't feel quite so bad. Not only the players but the fans appreciate the rich history of baseball in St. Louis and everyone at the vintage base ball games does what they can to preserve what they repeatedly remind you was "a gentleman's game."

Missouri was a tense place in 1860. Jayhawks were raiding into the farms and small towns along the state's western border. A new political party, the Republican Party, was gaining strength with their radical standard bearer, Abraham Lincoln. But there was still optimism as the St. Louis Massacre was yet a year away and it was said that the northern and southern sympathizers, Harney and Price, were working on an agreement to keep Missouri neutral should a full-fledged civil war erupt in the rest of the country. This was the setting when a Union soldier, Jerry Fruin, gathered a group of young men together in Lafayette Park to instruct them in a new game called base ball. This is the very park where they met and where Judge Shepard Barclay became St. Louis' first base ball organizer and promoter. (And, yes, baseball was two words back then.)

Today, that same park serves as the home field for the St. Louis Perfectos where they battle teams from across the Midwest. They share the park with the St. Louis Cyclones whose name is linked to an even older St. Louis team. Other local teams include the Unions from Jefferson Barracks and the

St. Louis Brown Stockings. (from Kirkwood) All teams are beautifully clad in bright uniforms of the day and many of the fans wear team colors to show their support. Of course the Perfectos wear cardinal red because the original perfectos would become the Cardinals. One modern invention helps the fans to enjoy the game more – the folding lawn chair. If you look closely, you will also see some modern coolers behind the team's bench.

Games are played by the rules from an official 1862 rule book. The vernacular sounds a little different to our modern ears. This'll help you to understand the 1860s terms being used.

- Ballist – the baseball player
- Arbiter – umpire
- Hurler – the pitcher
- Behind – the catcher
- Cranks, Rooters, & Bugs - the spectators
- Home Base – a one-foot
- Striker – the hitter
- Cloud Hunter – a fly ball
- Daisy Cutter – a ground ball
- Dead – out
- Hands Dead – number of outs
- Aces – single runs

Home Base / a one-foot diameter circular iron plate

- Bull Pen – where the cranks sit
- Muff – an error
- Muffin – a player who makes errors.
- The Garden – the outfield
- Scout – an outfielder
- Rover or Rover Scout – shortstop
- Tender – Baseman covering a particular
- Base: First, Second, Third.

So now, armed with a handful of these terms, you can fit right in with the other cranks and maybe one day even become a mascot (bat boy) or even a ballist. Of course then you would have to be known by some nickname like Cowpie, Hardwood, or Stubblefingers. Shortstop was a rover position in those days and could change his position on the field depending on who the striker happened to be. Much the same thing is accomplished today with "the shift." Tenders of first, second, and third bases however were required to remain within a two-foot radius of their base until the ball was hurled. Runners can steal bases at any time.

This "gentleman's game" is today played with both male and female players but, since no gloves are used, be prepared for jammed fingers and sore palms. Remember, it is also considered "un-gentlemanly" and in bad taste to try and trick a striker. The hurler throws dew drops (tosses the ball underhanded) so there is plenty of action and plenty of opportunities to "leg it." Bats are very similar to those used today and the balls are the same size and weight but stitched differently. They also tend to go soft very quickly.

In fact, the entire strategy of the game is different now from what they knew then. Whereas the modern game is, in large part, a contest between pitchers and hitters, one hundred and fifty years ago it was more of a contest between hitters and fielders. And, even more important then than now, you never want to chafe (complain to) the umpire. To do so will probably result in a very real fine.

Washington claims to have had the first Vintage Base Ball Assn. team in Missouri. It began in 2001. Its team, the Eagles, was joined by the Perfectos within weeks or even days of that 2001 beginning. The other St. Louis teams followed quickly along with other teams from across the Midwest.

In 1899 the original St. Louis Perfectos came to Washington for a game with the original Eagles. It must

~ 273 ~

have been something beautiful to watch those two good teams playing in this riverfront town next to the Busch Brewery. (Same Busch family – different brother) Perfectos from that era included the future Hall of Famers, Cy Young, Jesse Burkett and Bobby Wallace. While the Washington team is no more, they did play for a time and are remembered by many today.

The old style of base ball seems less competitive and a lot more fun. Teams sprung up all across this state and others. The stakes for winning were usually only the bragging rights and a beer purchased by the losing team. The beer leagues popularized the game as did the soldiers in their Civil War teams and the pioneers flooding westward from St. Louis, Independence, St. Joseph and the other gateway cities.

Going to a game? They are free but be sure and check the schedule on the web pages for the Perfectos, the Unions, the Brown Stockings or the Cyclones before you go. Games are played on Saturdays and usually at one o'clock. Tournaments often go all day long. These ballists and their cranks are also preservationists and seem eager to present a living museum activity to other towns and cities. Contact them if you would like to sponsor a game or tournament.

There are many places to watch or participate in vintage baseball games across Missouri, Illinois, Indiana, and Kansas but it is hard to imagine a more pleasant place than amid the ancient trees, and surrounded by the gracious Victorian town homes of the Lafayette Park neighborhood. After all, this is where base ball west of the Mississippi was first played and, with just a little imagination, it becomes wonderfully, colorfully, and charmingly visible again today.

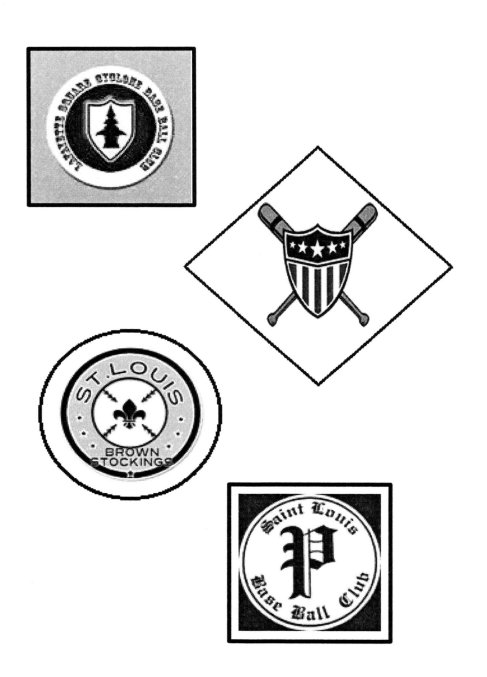

Creve Coeur Airport

Just west of Interstate 270 and near Creve Coeur Lake in Maryland Heights you will find an amazing place. The Creve Coeur Airport is home to over 75 privately-owned historic aircraft which are more than 45 years old. In the Historic Aircraft Restoration Museum they have over two dozen very old eye-popping airplanes. The unusual thing about these old planes is that they are all in flying condition.

When I say "flying condition" I really mean it. They are taken out and flown from time to time and some are even available for you to ride in. The cost is $100.00 but rising fuel prices may cause a slight increase.

Now these are old planes with cloth stretched over a framework and then painted and "doped" to form the wings and bodies. They have old tri-motors, racing planes, celebrity planes, airliners and more. There is one old airliner with wicker chairs for the passengers. Several of the planes were used by Charles Lindbergh. How about a Russian Aeroflot flying boat?

Over half of all the flying Monocoupes in the entire world are here. You will be amazed.

This is not a little building with some nice planes all lined up. It's a big place with aircraft crowded into many hangers. Therefore, it may not be the right experience for little children. But for many of us, it's a little peek at heaven. Be aware that this is not a normal tourist destination. It is a non-profit facility operated by pilots who have their own businesses and occupations. There is not always someone there to give a tour so you must call ahead. The number is (314) 878-9575.

Ferry Boats

When I was very young my parents said that we were going for a drive and would be riding on a ferry boat. Being very small, I was disappointed when we arrived and rode across a river on a little flat boat with a gasoline motor. I had been expecting a "Fairy Boat" to be pulled by some little winged people. I tell you this to make the point that many children have never had this experience and may not know what a ferry is.

Missouri's river towns and cities used to have their own ferries across the many rivers of the state but our wealth permitted the building of bridges in many of the most important places. Still there are some places where crossing the river is impossible without some help.

One of my favorite ferries is a tiny little boat that takes two or three cars across the Gasconade at a time. I mentioned this in my section about the River's Edge Restaurant. This **Fredericksburg Ferry** has been in operation since 1886 but today it is not a very profitable operation and sometimes it just doesn't operate. As this book is compiled it is not running and the people of the area are hoping that someone will purchase it and operate it just for the love of the unique enterprise.

Ferry Boats (cont.)

Another good little ferry is the **Akers Ferry**. It crosses the Current River near Salem and connects Routes K with KK. This one is really tiny, folks, and a real change from those big ones on the Mississippi and Missouri Rivers. This one is also in a very scenic place. Refer back to this book's sections on the Grist Mills.

The **Golden Eagle Ferry** is a big, safe, fun boat across the Mississippi River connecting St. Charles County with the little town of Golden Eagle in Illinois. It's popular and busy so plan to get in line and wait for a while on some days. From St. Charles, take highway 94 north and watch closely for the County Road B sign which takes you to the Golden Eagle.

If you liked you could usually journey a little north and cross back into Missouri on the Winfield Ferry. At this writing the Winfield Ferry is closed but plans are underway to reopen. You can always cross the Illinois into Grafton on the Grafton Ferry. From there it is a short trip down to Alton. Just before you get to Alton, look for the Piassa creature painted on the bluffs. Marquette and Joliet wrote about this in their journals.

Ferry Boats (cont.)

The Canton Riverfront is the place to meet the **Canton Ferry**. It will take your car across the river to Meyer, Illinois. It carries bicycles, semi-trucks and anything in between. It has been making this run since 1853 and is the oldest ferry operation on the Mississippi. This one is a toll ferry.***

***NOTE:* At the time this Second Edition is being prepared, the ferry boat at Canton is out of service. It is this writer's belief that it will not resume service at any time.

The **Ste. Genevieve-Madoc Ferry** runs from Ste. Gen's Little Rock Landing to the Illinois side known at the Madoc Landing. It is near Highways 3 and 155 on that shore. It runs every fifteen minutes or so. To get on board, follow North Main St. for about 1½ miles north from town. This one also charges a small fee.

Ferry Boats (cont.)

The Dorena-Hickman Ferry crosses the Mississippi between Dorena, MO and Hickman, KY. Take Highway A south from Dorena to catch the boat. This is another big one and the usual toll for cars is $14.00. Once in Kentucky, I suggest that you take any of the nearby highways north and cross the Ohio into Cairo, Illinois. I am not suggesting that you spend any time in Cairo but, if you look at a map, you will see that Cairo is a very unusual peninsula sticking down between the Mississippi and the Ohio.

At the tip of this tiny peninsula and just south of Cairo's business district there is a unique little park. Climb the little tower and look around. It's wonderful. To your left is the gigantic Ohio River and to your right is the even-larger Mississippi. Both of the rivers are filled with huge tows of barges lining the banks and more barges plying the rivers both north and south. It's a wonderful place like no other.

Then, as you leave the park you can get right on the big bridge and cross over into Missouri on US Highways 60 and 62. At this point you're just nine miles from Charleston and two Interstate Highways.

Hannibal

First, a warning. Many children these days have not heard of Tom Sawyer or Huckleberry Finn. This is especially true of children nine and under. You cannot expect them to share your excitement or enthusiasm about the haunts of these characters. Before you take children you must acquaint them with Mark Twain's stories. If you don't want to read one of the modern sanitized politically correct books, then at least watch a watered-down movie.

Then your fourth-grade-or-older children will understand what they are experiencing – and there is a lot to experience here. The town has done a remarkable job of blending convenient parking, modern amenities and quaint historic buildings. Start near Tom's house at the Visitor's Center. Send the kids to the bathroom while you grab a map and plan your visit.

Everyone visits Tom's House, Becky's House, and the Tom and Huck Statue. And, of course, they should. Don't miss those! However, too many people miss some of the other parts of the stories that are important to the kids. For instance, I guarantee that every child who knows Twain's stories loves the scary part about Tom and Becky being lost in the cave and encountering Injun Joe. That cave is there and it's an easy tour. You really should do that. By the way, this cave has the distinction of being America's very first show cave.

Further, I want to remind you that the central part of every Twain story is the Mighty Mississippi. Yet, some people come to town and see the two houses then head back out to the highway. Please take time to visit Riverview Park and feel the size and power of that river. Stop to imagine three people out on that current in a little raft.

Now, after the Titanic movie and the Broadway play, many people are familiar with the rags to riches story of the lady known as the Unsinkable Molly Brown. Of course her real name was Margaret Tobin and now her home in Hannibal is open as a museum. It's an Irish immigrant's cottage from the 1860s.

What else? The trolley, the riverboat, the miniature train museum, water play at Mark Twain's Landing? Oh, there's lots more! I want to suggest a very inexpensive afternoon or evening watching some talented young men playing baseball and hoping to get picked up by someone from the Majors.

Caveman baseball is popular with the locals and for good reason – They have a lot of fun. There is also some very good history at their ballpark, Clemons Field. In days gone by Clemens Field was the home of many good minor league and semi-pro teams including this writer's favorite, Hannibal's Cannibals. While you're sitting there in the beautiful old white stone stadium look around you and try to imagine the scene as it would have been in the early 1940s. This was the location of one of Missouri's Prisoner of War camps.

This area has several good bed and breakfasts. For a time in the 1800s, this was Missouri's second-largest city and the homes and buildings from that era reflect the importance and the prosperity of the place. You might even want to look into some of the beautiful old antebellum houses on the hill because some of them are truly treasures in need of some T.L.C. Ever thought about starting a B&B of your own?

I strongly urge you to include the free Hannibal History Museum right there in the middle of the old Main Street business district. Besides being a very good museum, it's ground zero for many of the town's special events and festivals. If you like street fairs, Twain on Main is hard to beat and the Museum provides clean free restrooms instead of the usual festival event porta-potties. So with or without the kids, take your camera and make this trip that everyone owes to himself or herself. There is so much here that you can tailor your trip to your own likes and interests.

Tom and Becky at Twain on Main

Heartland Dairies

Up where Shelby, Knox, and Lewis Counties all meet there is a most unique farm that is open and welcoming to visitors. With 4500 cows being milked and thousands more in the field, this is the state's largest dairy farm. They even milk a large herd of about 1200 goats. They invite visitors there to watch as they milk about 350 cows per hour. If you visit, your favorite place here will be the nursery center. You can watch all of this from an observation deck.

This is not a petting zoo. It is a very modern highly-productive working farm. It employs many Missourians from the northeastern part of the state. In addition to those area folks, it employs about 60 people at a time who are in various stages of recovery from their own personal problems. The goal is to give these people confidence and a solid work ethic. So far, this has been a very effective program.

To find the farm you must get to the area of La Belle or Newark, Missouri. From either Highway 6 or Highway 156, you just turn on County Road D and watch for the Heartland Dairy sign.

Mansfield

When Laura Ingalls married Almonzo Wilder they were way out in South Dakota. And, while Laura did enjoy her father's taste for change and frontier adventure, she also enjoyed the town life that she had only sampled. So the newlyweds moved back toward a more settled place. The Ingalls family had lived near Independence, Kansas and she thought that just a little farther east would be just about right. They drove their wagon to Springfield which they loved but they were still looking for a smaller homier hometown. Then they found Mansfield.

They bought land and built a big two-story frame house on a rocky outcropping just east of town. They named this place the Rocky Ridge Ranch and here they spent the rest of their lives. Luckily for Laura, she found a job in Mansfield's Library and, during Story Hour, she would tell the children and staff about her adventures growing up in all of those little houses across the frontier. The library staff encouraged her to write the stories down and submit them to some magazines. The classic snowball effect took place when the public latched on to those stories and soon Laura and her daughter, Rose, were publishing books about their lives. One of the books describes the first four years of their lives in Mansfield.

Rocky Ridge Ranch

When you are in South Central Missouri you must stop and visit the Rocky Ridge. There is a small admission charge to tour the house but this only helps to maintain the home and property. The little souvenir shop is welcoming and interesting.

Old pictures show that Mansfield still has some of the same buildings and features that Laura and Almonzo would have seen all those decades ago and, as in most small Missouri towns there is a little café serving basic good food to the local farmers and businessmen. You might want to take a few minutes and have lunch or a snack and soak in the atmosphere.

If you're really lucky, you might meet a local couple with a traveling barbeque pit who set up in a different location around the area on different days of the week. Vance and Cindy usually come to Mansfield one day each week. On those days, you'll want to get the barbeque. If you want, get Vance to tell you about why his cooking is so much better than most. He's happy to let you know everything about it.

Now, if you really want a feel for how the place must have been when Laura and Almonzo arrived, you need to go just a little north of town. Gardeners are familiar with the Baker Creek Heirloom Seeds and this is their home. The Baker Creek people have, right there on their property, something called Bakersville Pioneer Village. When the original version of this book was published, this little treasure was almost undiscovered. Now it is a destination for many gardeners from many points of the map. Anyone who loves gardening will love this place! Anything you would expect to find in a frontier farming village is here and, of course, they have those seeds and produce. Bring your toe-tappin' shoes because they even have live music and feeling "tappy-toed" is perfectly normal.

If you happen to crave a quiet family-friendly place to spend a few days, this community has a place called Mansfield Woods. The setting is pure Ozark hills, valleys, and ponds. The cabins are rustic but modern with air-conditioning, kitchenettes, and such, but the really distinctive things about this place are outside. Hicks Cave is right on the premises. It's not a commercial cave but it is large and accessible and inviting. A great place if you and the kids are up for some low-key adventure. Lifelong memories are made in places like this. Mansfield Woods has some other nice surprises for you to discover when you get there. You won't be disappointed.

Just a stone's throw from Mansfield Woods is something called Laura's Memories. This is an outdoor "pageant" performed by the Ozark Mountain Players and it depicts pioneer life and Laura Ingalls Wilder. Here's the catch though: They only do their performances six times a year. You will want to check their webpage and plan ahead.

Marshall

Whenever I think of Marshall I automatically think of Jim the Wonder Dog. Jim was probably the most intelligent non-human who ever lived. If you are not familiar with his feats, please take the time to look him up or read about him in my previous book, *Tales From Missouri and the Heartland*. After you do, you will want to visit the dog's statue here in his home town.

Jim the Wonder Dog

And if you're an airplane lover you will want to tour the Nicholas Beazeley Air Museum. This is here for two reasons.

You see in days gone by, Marshall's Flying School was the largest civilian flying school in the world. Over 3000 people graduated from this place. The second reason is that the Nicholas-Beazeley Aircraft Corporation built many fine planes here.

Maybe more than any other city, Marshall is one in which you need to plan ahead. They host a huge variety of special events and you will be well-advised to shop before you go. By that I mean to choose the events that most suit your preferences. **Here are a few of the best:**

Viking Stampede Rodeo	State Cornhusking Championship
Country Patchwork Quilt Guild Show	Santa Fe Trail Days
Bear Creek Blues Festival (at Slater)	Saline County Fair

The Market on the Square provides fresh fruits, vegetables, crafts, and more but this is seasonal and not every day. This produce doesn't come from Guatemala – It's seasonal. Once again, you will want to plan ahead. The Marshall Community Band provides free concerts on the beautiful courthouse lawn every Tuesday evening all through the summer. What a great way to finish your day in this pleasant town. (Bring a lawn chair.)

New Haven

New Haven's place in history is assured by one of its early residents. John Colter was an important person on the Lewis and Clark Expedition. As he journeyed upstream he saw this place and remembered it as his chosen spot to settle. Of course he did. He and his Osage wife have left generations who still gather here in great reunions at the John Colter Memorial on the Riverfront.

Colter was one of our nation's greatest explorers and discovered a place so exotic that most people refused to believe his accounts and descriptions could be real. Those who thought there might be some truth in his stories named the place Colter's Hell. Later it became the world's first national park and we came to know it by its Indian name, Yellowstone. You wouldn't want to tell the kids you were taking them to Colter's Hell, would you?

When the War of 1812 erupted, John Colter joined another area resident, Nathan Boone to form a military unit. It was at this time that Colter became ill and died. His friend,

Nathan Boone saw to his burial on a high bluff overlooking the Missouri. Later his stone and bones were ground into gravel as the railroad widened its roadbed.

German immigrants helped settle the area through the 19th century, many of them coming from the Borgholzhausen, Germany area in the state of North Rhine-Westphalia. These Germans have left us many fine wineries all along the Missouri Valley here in what many call the Missouri Rhine. The best known local vintner is probably the Röbller Vineyard and Winery.

As a history buff, I love the things mentioned above. However, here is what I think visitors will take away from New Haven. First is the unique physical appearance of the place. It's all about hills here. The streets are narrow and curving. The parts of town are connected with incredible sets of concrete stairways. The churches and homes are perched on the steep hills giving them a different look than you see in your hometown.

Second is the river. You can't actually see the river as you drive through town. However, if you get out at the Colter Memorial, you can take a few steps upward onto the levee and find a paved walkway that leads you along the river where eagles often dive catching the aquatic bounty. On the other side (town side) of the levee are several small and very nice bed and breakfast establishments with free access to the levee and its park benches.

The third thing to love in New Haven is the Walt. A very tiny old movie theater is still showing movies to teenagers and nostalgic older folks. This labor of love was refurbished by a couple who kept everything as historically accurate as possible. They even found a scrap of the original carpet (under the candy counter) and had a new carpet woven just like the original. Of course it was named for Walt Disney. Let's get some Junior Mints and watch a flick at the Walt!

Augusta

 A friend in St. Louis told me that when a couple wants to make a rendezvous and not be seen by other friends they meet at the Wineries in Augusta. The same things that attract them attract many other people. Beautiful river town scenery, excellent wineries, quaint old buildings, the Katy Trail, great B & Bs, and a new microbrewery.

This town started because of the excellent landing spot right on the Missouri. Today, however, you'll not find that spot because the river has moved itself to the far side of the valley. This left the area with many square miles of rich bottom land. What would Lewis and Clark think of the rich farmland where their river used to be?

Speaking of the Voyage of Discovery, when the expedition headed west up the big river, they encountered a small village here which they recorded as La Charrette. In fact it was the last trace of European civilization that the explorers saw and the first place they stopped on their homeward journey. The little fortified village was established here in 1762 and was washed away in the floods of 1842 and 1843. A La Charrette marker remains in Marthasville's Wessel Park

Architectural historian Crosby Brown discovered the remains of the fort. It yielded enough information that he was able to restore it. However, he rebuilt it on the more populous and higher south side of the river near Washington, MO. Today, the restored trading post houses is a collection of 18th- and 19th-century artifacts and is furnished accordingly. It has a trade room, a blacksmith's shop and a recreation of frontier living quarters. The modern Fort Charrette trading post is open for tours and there is no admission price but donations are encouraged. As this Second Edition is being prepared, the writer wants to caution you that Mr. Brown's health has been poor but he is improving. His Fort Charrette is worth visiting but don't be too disappointed if you find it closed on some days.

The Plein Air Art Event might be the biggest event in this little town. It's a ten day visual art fair with many artists painting at their chosen locations. At this writing, the event takes place in mid-April but that is subject to change.

So, what can a village of 300 offer visitors? The answer might include generous doses of history, scenery, wineries, antiquing, and a pleasant relaxed atmosphere just minutes away from Interstate highways and suburban St. Louis. In warm seasons the rows of vines covering the hills is truly beautiful.

Clinton

If you found yourself in the area of Clinton in the old days, you were probably on your way to somewhere. This place was on several trails going especially southward and westward. The location of the town's courthouse square is the highest point in the area and was a natural campsite for early wagon trains and for Natives before that. Even today Clinton is at the junction of three state highways. Any route into town will also remind you that there were three railroads here for many years.

By 1837 two log buildings were already erected on the square. The first was a storehouse and the second was a tavern and hotel. It was a dogtrot cabin called Pollard's Tavern. One observer said the hotel/tavern, "was a first-class structure and looked a good deal like a cattle pen." It was also 1837 when money was allocated for a courthouse building on the square.

Soon Clinton boasted its first two-story house, the Dorman House, which is open to the public today. Across the street there was a stage coach stop. At least one Civil War skirmish took place on the lawn of the Dorman House.

Things really began to pop in 1870 when the first train arrived. This city grew 450% in the 1870s because of the railroad. This was the time when the city began to fill with three-story Victorian homes and many of those are still standing.

Today the courthouse on the square is the one built in 1892 and it's made of Warrensburg sandstone. Looking at it from across the street, you might think that it is impressive but it looks like something is missing. You would be right. Originally there was a 127 foot tower on the top. Within months of completion the tower began to leak and was causing water damage to the rest of the structure. The architect could not fix the problem so the tower was removed. Now it stands as a very impressive structure on the largest town square in the entire state.

Both Yankee & Reb at Civil War Memorial

In 1913 a Clinton high school student, Royal Booth, wanted to try his hand at poultry husbandry. Starting with a handful of eggs and a little incubator, he built a gigantic hatchery operation which was copied by others in town and soon Clinton was exporting four million chicks a year! Eventually this town exported 110 million baby chicks in one year. You can read more about Clinton's and other Missouri Hatcheries in *Tales From Missouri and the Heartland*.

I invite the visitor to begin your tour on the Courthouse Square. Note the Civil War Memorial which remembers men from both sides of the conflict. Very unusual! On the southeast corner of the lawn is a reminder that just a century ago horses were still a part of everyday life. A very nice watering trough stands there as a reminder of the way things were in 1910 or so. On the northwest corner of the lawn is a wonderful bandstand from 1921. It has been remodeled twice and it still used for concerts, speeches, rallies or whatever the citizens need. On September 11, 2011 the town dedicated a memorial on the southwest corner of the lawn. This memorial includes steel from the World Trade Center.

Just a few steps from the square is the Henry County Museum and Cultural Arts Center. You don't like those kinds of places? I strongly urge you to visit this building. This is the old Anheuser-Busch Building and much of that operation remains. The front offices, stables, bottling rooms, stables, and coolers are still there. The museum is actually a complex of buildings ranging from the main building to a dog trot cabin. There are varied exhibits and a great resource for genealogists. It is this writer's opinion that Washington, Warrenton, and Clinton are the three Missouri cities with the best collections of amateur historians and they provide the three best historical museums. You must visit what Clinton offers you.

Downtown DeSoto (Remember when Chrysler made the DeSoto automobile?) is a special place. This restored auto dealership houses a private collection of vintage cars beautifully restored. You will love this!

As you look at Clinton's downtown buildings take special note of how the old and new buildings blend. This is no accident. Clintonites have made a special effort to make their very modern buildings capture the architectural aspects of the buildings from decades and centuries past. The Delozier Building on the corner is a special gem.

I'm sure you remember the June day in 2006 when an 1800s era building on the square collapsed with fifty Elks Club members inside. That is a wound still healing in this town of 9400 but a large red brick complex has already taken its place on the site.

Today people come to Clinton to work at the Rival Crock Pot factory or any number of good employers. Others come to Clinton for access to Truman Lake. And, of course, this is the beginning/end of the Katy Trail. If you find yourself in Clinton for any reason at all you will want to have a bite at the Ben Franklin Bistro. It's a coffee house which resides on the square in the old Ben Franklin Store building.

Galena

Any Missouri fourth grader will tell you that galena is Missouri's official state mineral. It's iron ore and the heavy black shiny rock is what brought the very first European settlers to our state. The great explorer Henry Schoolcraft came through this place in 1818 and wrote of finding galena laying across the ground. But I'm getting ahead of my own story.

First populated in 7000 B.C. by Ozark Bluff Dweller Indians, the Osage were here when white men arrived. Later Delaware tribes were settled here until being moved in 1929. All of these populations and the Europeans who followed chose to settle along the fresh waters of the James River.

Mr. Louis Stanley, a respected local historian told a story about the Galena neighborhood. He told that "just downstream from the hollow, there was a ford across Beaver Creek used by many travelers going from east to west. Once, a long time ago, a group of Spaniards were crossing Beaver at this point when they were attacked by unknown assailants. They were carrying with them gold and silver bars and Spanish coins." It is said that Mr. Stanley found some gold coins near this spot and some people claim to have seen the coins before they were destroyed in a fire. It was rumored that the gold and silver were buried nearby, or lost in the stream. Do you own a metal detector?

James Yocum (sometimes spelled Yoachum) of French origin was the first white settler in the area. In about 1790 located at the junction of James and White rivers. He carried on trading with the Indians and later with the white settlers. He traded goods (mostly furs and pelts) for other necessities such as coffee, salt, blankets, cloth, shoes, rifles, bullets, pots, knives, hatchets, axes that could be found nowhere else in the area.

Some historians write that this settler/trader issued his own trade-coin, the Yocum Dollar. This coin was stamped with two words, "Yocum Dollar", and was not considered counterfeit. In fact, while its size and shape were identical to the American dollar, it contained more pure silver than an actual dollar so it was actually worth more. Some historians deny the coin's existence. None are known to exist at this time.

In 1851 Stone County was organized and Jamestown was named as the County Seat. But when the new county was named it was also decided to change the name of the county seat from Jamestown to Galena.

This writer has pleasant memories of the schools and school staffs that I dealt with in Stone County and the neighboring Taney County. You can't help being struck by the quality of the people in these institutions. I hold a theory that rural places may offer less opportunity for economic advancement so the best people in the community are attracted to places like the schools for employment. I greatly appreciate the adults in the schools and the students constantly demonstrate the products of the teaching efforts. I must also mention that these schools have little money but they "make do."

One of the fine sights to see in Galena is a bridge over the James River which is closed to auto traffic. This graceful structure has been saved as a pedestrian bridge because of its historic significance. Its five arches stretch for 764 feet across the river valley so it's a beauty. But it is special for two other reasons. It is a perfect example of a new modern style (modern for 1927) bridge built to be beautiful in its simplicity. The other reason is that it is built in the shape of a "Y." How many bridges have you seen with a "Y" shape? So, stop for a minute and take a walk across the beautiful valley on the Galena Bridge. If you decide to dip your toes in the clear waters below, you'll be the better for it.

<u>Frohna</u>

Wittenberg, Dresden, Seelitz, Altenburg, Johannesberg, & Uniontown (Paitzdorf)

In 1839 when more than 500 immigrants from Saxony landed in Wittenberg, Missouri. The group spread into the surrounding wilderness and started farms, businesses and the seven German towns named above. They were from the area of Bremen and staunch Lutherans in their beliefs. Because of this, three of their first acts were to build churches, start a seminary, and to establish the Lutheran Church, Missouri Synod.

Not much remains of that landing spot or even of Wittenberg itself but there is an important marker there given by the Perry County Lutherans to show where the church once stood. It should be noted that the Wittenberg residents, because of their work ethic, thrived but the town was washed away by floods in 1927, 1973, and 1993.

I want to strongly encourage everyone in Missouri to visit The Saxon Lutheran Memorial at Frohna. It is an outdoor museum in the form of a log cabin village located on the farm of an early pioneer. It has much to tell us about the beginnings of the Lutheran Church in our state but also about the beginning of the state itself. This is not a public property but a private project of a group of citizens. The museum is open Tuesdays through Saturdays as well as Sunday afternoons from March through December. There is no admission fee but a freewill donation is appreciated.

It is important that you call ahead so the curator, Linda Lorenz, can have sufficient staff on hand to assist visitors. The number is 573-824-5404. It's easy to find buy going to Frohna and looking for 296 Saxon Memorial Drive. Ms. Lorenz says, "I invite you to come by and visit this amazing site, where you can learn something new by seeing something old." I suggest that you bring your camera – this countryside place is beautiful.

El Dorado Springs

As such things go, El Dorado Springs is a late-comer. It wasn't founded until 1881 so it didn't suffer in the same way that other area towns. It literally sprung up because of the spring discovered in 1881 and that is also how the town got its name. Of course the Osage already knew about the spring and they not only camped here but they bathed their ills in the restorative waters. Soon after 1881 the healthful waters were being shipped all over the world.

In 1896 something special happened. A group of young men formed a community band and they have been playing ever since. As far as any records can show, this is the oldest continuous municipal band in the United States. This band still plays in the bandstand three times per week all through the warm weather months. Why don't you plan to be there for one of their concerts? If you do, be sure to check out the bandstand made of native stones. The tops of its walls are decorated with those round rocks we talked about in the very first story.

An even better thing might be finding yourself in El Dorado Springs near July 20th when the town hosts the Annual Picnic. That way you get the band and lots more besides. It is claimed that this picnic began the very year that the city was formed so it is one of the oldest continuous events in the state.

In order to fit in you will want to pronounce the name of the place like a native. They say: *'el du RAY doh springs'*. Many just call the town Eldo, pronounced *EL doe*. They'll make you welcome even if you say it wrong.

Saint Mary

Originally known as Sainte Marie's Landing, this tiny town became with time, Iron Mountain City, Yankeetown, Camp Rowdy, Saint Mary's, Saint Mary's and now, Saint Mary.

In 1876 this place had four general stores, four hotels, and manufacturers of flour, cigars, and wagons. Of course there were all of the service industry craftsmen and professionals needed to serve the 500 residents plus the regular river boats and stage coaches. Then in 1881 the Mississippi changed its course and left a 1500 acre island between the town and its river lifeblood. The island of course is Kaskaskia and is actually a part of Illinois even though it's on our side of the river. If you're in St. Mary, why not drive a little east and see all of the Illinois license plates on the western side of the Big Muddy.

One remnant of the glory days is a large white frame bluff-top home. Now known as White Cliff Manor, it's an up-scale bed and breakfast with wonderful views and quiet elegance. Other than its interesting history and an excellent B

& B, there's not much to talk about in St. Mary. But – I really like this place. I think the folks who live here are very happy to be doing so. A visitor here will always be recognized as such but will be made welcome and maybe that's why I feel the way I do. Hospitality is rarer these days and therefore, more valuable when you find it.

Louisiana

"Have you heard tell of Sweet Betsy from Pike? She crossed the wide prairie with old Uncle Ike, two yoke of cattle, a large yeller dog, a tall Shanghai rooster, and a one-spotted hog." Remember that song? Well, the pioneering Betsy and her uncle were from Pike County which has been important in Missouri's story. Another example comes from the Honey War in which the troops from Iowa spotted some Pike County Missourians and corrupted the word Pike into a derogatory name and Missouri was known by some as the Puke State. If you're not familiar with this, read my *Tales From Missouri and the Heartland*.

Louisiana is one of the early gems of Pike County. The first settlers in this immediate area arrived in 1808 and Fort Buffalo was built by 1812 to protect residents during the War of 1812 from the British and their Indian allies. The first home in what would become the actual town was built in 1817 and the next year Louisiana became the county seat. Later the county courts moved to Bowling Green.

The little village grew and prospered as a center of agriculture and commerce on the riverside. Then the railroads by-passed the town and went through St. Louis and Hannibal instead. That began the gradual shrinking of the town's population and prosperity. In 1880 the population was 7,000 and now it's a little over half that.

During all of those years when the town was shrinking, something big was growing. In fact at the time when the town was being laid out, Judge James Hart Stark was laying out his orchards. By grafting his fruit trees to the roots of native crabapples he created new varieties and became the largest mail-order nursery in the world. This, of course, you recognize as the Stark Bros. Nurseries. One of the original log cabins built by Judge Stark is still there at the nursery.

So why visit Louisiana? For one thing it's on the Great River Road which is famous for its beautiful scenery, its bald eagle watching, and its history. Missouri's Department of Natural Resources has credited Louisiana with, "the most intact Victorian Streetscape in the state of Missouri." The Georgia Street Historic District has over 54 buildings in the downtown area. There are antebellum homes in the Italianate and Victorian styles. Many are listed on the National Register. You might like to tour these homes in October during the Great Mansions and Estate Tour. Reminder – The scenery here in October is gorgeous!

Louisiana has three natural parks and, of course, the magnificent riverfront. What is labeled the "50 Miles of Art Corridor" includes the homes and studios of accomplished artists and craftspeople in Louisiana and her sister cities of Hannibal and Clarksville. Wait until you see the murals and sculptures on open display here.

I suggest that, when you visit, you bring a picnic lunch or buy one at one of the good little restaurants in town. Then go to Riverfront Park or to either of the scenic overlooks on Highway 79 north of town. Let the peace, serenity, and grandeur of the scenery soak in.

Herculaneum

When Lewis and Clark made their way up the Mississippi prior to their Voyage of Discovery, they made note of a settlement of Americans on Joachim Creek. They called it "Swacken Creek" and others called it "Swashin Creek" but this was the place. We know that there was a settlement here prior to 1803 because it is recorded that in 1798 the first Protestant Sermon west of the Mississippi was delivered at Bates Rock.

In 1808 Moses Austin actually laid out and founded the town along with his teenage son, Stephen Austin and business partner, Samuel Hammond. The Austins would go on to found Potosi and then lead Missourians to start the Republic of Texas. When the post office was established in 1811 the town was described as having twenty houses, two hundred residents and several businesses. In 1817 the first steamboat on the upper Mississippi (the Zebulon Pike) stopped at Herculaneum and nothing would be the same from that point onward.

In 1809 a shot tower was built atop the bluffs at Herculaneum. By 1813 two others were in place and turning out shot. The war of 1812 made it abundantly clear how important it was to have the area's lead quickly turned into good quality ammunition. The name of "shot" tower is a little misleading because these things didn't just produce the pellets for shot guns but also the larger round bullets for the rifles of that time. They even produced some gigantic spheres of lead which were then used as cannonballs.

The molten lead would drop through copper sieves (thus creating the various exact sizes) and fall through the air from three-story buildings (towers) above the bluffs. As the drops fell, they naturally formed into to round balls of lead and then splashed into shallow water directly below. Here they collected and cooled. From there the balls were taken to another building to be rounded and smoothed. The result was a perfectly round object ready for hunting, warfare, or sport.

The Original Shot Tower at Herculaneum, circa 1809

In 1819 Austin and Hammond sold the entire town for $50. Austin saw the layered limestone bluffs and thought they looked like the amphitheater seats which had been uncovered following an eruption of Vesuvius. You remember that one of the buried towns was Pompeii and the one with the amphitheater was Herculaneum. This is why he assigned the name to this place.

Another interesting thing happened concerning these limestone formations. In 1919 the St. Louis Zoo wanted to construct new and natural bear pits so they came to Herculaneum and made plaster casts of the cliffs. Then they poured concrete into the casts and got the bear pit bluffs that we see today.

Since the late 1700s this place has been steadily employed at taking minerals from the earth and transporting them to market. But it wasn't until 1972 that the city officially became incorporated as a fourth-class city. That same year the first two police officers were hired. And that same year residents were reminded of their heritage as 1000-year-old Indian burial mounds were unearthed. Four years later, in 1976, home delivery of the U.S. Mail began for the first time in "Hercky."

Some good clean fun began in 1994. Every year since then the city and its fire department have sponsored the Jeffco

Fire Engine Rally. They parade gigantic new trucks, antique equipment like hand-powered pumpers, fire dogs, and all sorts of mascot-type characters.

St. Louis has its arch and Kansas City has it fountains but Herculaneum has its 550 foot monster of a monument. This giant smokestack was erected by the Doe Run Company and it can be seen from everywhere. To give you an idea, this tower is exactly the same size at the Washington Monument!

People from outside the area will tell you that the smokestack is dead and gone. After all, the Doe Run Smelter closed its operation in 2013. Well, the chimney's demise has been greatly exaggerated. It stands! Now there are two things to know if you would like to see the giant. First is that it will eventually be brought down. You had better visit soon. The second thing is that, if you keep your ears open, you will be able to find out when it is destroyed. Wouldn't it be something to see that thing fall?

When you visit Herculaneum you will want to take in the scenery. Not just the rolling hills and trees but the views of the river and the countryside. You must go to the Dunklin-Fletcher Memorial Park on Main Street or the Governor Daniel Dunklin Grave Historic Site. These two Governors from Herculaneum posthumously provide some pleasant sightseeing on your daytrip.

Nevada

One cannot speak of Nevada (pronounced nuh VAY duh) without remembering two things. One is the War Between the States and the other is the town's women. In the 1850s and 1860s newspapers back east often wrote of "Bleeding Kansas" but, as I pointed out earlier, most of the bleeding was done on the Missouri side. Here in Vernon County there lived a number of immigrants from the south and a number who had been run out of Kansas by the Jayhawks.

Raids from neighboring Kansas were a constant worry but the folks in Vernon County were also under pressure from Union sympathizers just to the east in Cedar County. With pressure from both east and west, life was very precarious.

Feelings leaned southward when the actual war began but I think we could say that it was fear and outrage that finally forced the area's men to join into groups that came to be known as Bushwhackers. Fear from the pressures mentioned earlier and outrage over what some called the Camp Jackson Massacre or what most call the St. Louis Massacre. These things caused two immediate results.

The first was that hundreds of local men joined the pro-Southern forces and the second was that Union troops from Cedar County swept in and burned the town of Nevada to the ground. Only the school and the jail were spared. With nothing left to defend, the population moved out. It's Ironic that when the notorious Order No. 11 was issued It called for northern Vernon County to be burned but, in fact, there was nothing left there to burn.

If you remember, I mentioned that the local women were noteworthy. During the War Nevada had a good number of what were called "Lady Bushwhackers" who, for the most part, served in non-combat roles but were helpful in many ways just the same. When Union troops were dispatched to set up picket posts guarding various river crossings, one observer noted that the Union soldiers paid far more attention to the rebel girls than to the rebel boys. As a result, about ten of the Union soldiers were "captured" by the Lady Bushwhackers and they settled to raise families in the area at war's end.

The women also deserve recognition for founding Cottey College in 1884. This is the only college in America which was founded by, operated for, and governed by women. It also happens to be a darned good school.

Three years later, in 1887, an interesting thing happened. Well-drillers tapped into a sulfur spring which soon created a lake. Locals created a park (Radio Park) around the lake and advertised for people to come and partake of their radioactive water. I suppose some of the things we do today will sound just as silly in the future.

Silly maybe, but Radio Park is a pleasant place as is the town square and the beautiful courthouse. The buildings on the square are from the peaceful time after the war and they reflect the 1870s and 1880s very well. Cottey College is a picturesque small campus with charming buildings and a pleasant place to stroll. And, remember from the earlier article, three miles north of town there is a giant morel mushroom. You will never forgive yourself if you miss that. Today this town is about as nice as a place can be while being so close to Kansas.

Tipton

In the 1830s William Tipton Seely arrived in this place with land grants earned in the War of 1812. Some of the grants were his and some he had purchased from other veterans. He established a trading post and named the place Round Hill.

It was on a stage coach route running from Jefferson City to Wichita. He immediately began lobbying for a road running north to the river port at Boonville. Of course, his middle name became the name for the new town whose very beginning was tied to transportation.

On March 1, 1858, Seely began selling lots in the new town and by August there were already 250 residents. With dreams of possible railroads in the future the town boomed. Railroads arrived in 1858 and were to play a larger role in the community than anyone could have imagined. The trains traveled to Boonville and back every morning and then made a similar run to Versailles every afternoon.

Because of the trains Tipton quickly became a thriving town with Wells Fargo, The U.S. Express, stagecoaches, and heavy freight wagons coming here for mail, passengers and heavy freight all brought in by the railroad. You see, the boats and/or trains would bring the mail from the east all the way to Tipton.

In 1858 John Butterfield started the Butterfield Overland Mail Service which was a huge stage coach operation to carry the mail and even some passengers from Tipton to California and points in between. This business, by opening day, had 250 Concord coaches, 500 other vehicles including different kinds of coaches, 1800 horses, 1200 workers, and much, much more all operating out of Tipton.

Even today, it's still transportation that brings people to Tipton. What would those old-timers have thought of heated air-conditioned cars and paved highways? When they were trying desperately to get news from one place to another, what would they think of you listening to the world's news in your car? Highways 5 and 50 connect Tipton with Jeff City, Sedalia and the Lake of the Ozarks.

Back in 1891 Tipton resident, W. H. Coleman took some medicine which made him turn blue. He sued the manufacturer and was awarded $10,000 which he used to build a beautiful home on East Morgan. In 1916 Sterling Price James bought the home and in 1981 his family left the mansion to the city. Today it is the Sterling Price James Library and Museum. It has some small but interesting displays about the history of the town and of Moniteau County.

At some time when you're here, you will want to visit the Vanilla Grill. Good food and good ice cream in a pleasant setting. What would the stagecoach passengers have thought of a place like this?

Viburnum

I don't know of any attractions to draw you into the little town of Viburnum but It is just surrounded by natural attractions of every kind. Because of its location, however, you will probably travel through Viburnum as you go to these various places and I would like for you to know what a unique place this is.

Back in the 1830s the government wanted people to settle in the area but almost no one wanted to make this their home. Land prices were slashed and finally people began to purchase homesteads at $1.25 per acre. These folks usually came in small groups of family and friends who preferred a clannish isolated life of hunting and small farming operations. The abundant lumber provided a cash crop when people wanted and then minerals like iron and lead were discovered in the late 1880s.

So try to picture this. It is the early 1950s and the virgin timber is gone and a scraggly new-growth forest is springing up. Hogs, cattle and horses are allowed to roam wild through the countryside and harvested when needed. The Viburnum community is down to four houses, one of them was a 12 X 12 foot building.

Then the St. Joe Company came in to mine and smelt lead. In 1957 they laid out a new Viburnum and that is what you see today. Wide residential streets with trees down the middle, modern homes, attractive schools, and several prosperous churches. This is a new and modern town in the middle of a fairly isolated area. So the next time you find yourself driving through the Mark Twain National Forest, consider swinging over onto Highway 49 and check out this unique little town.

Licking

Being in the middle of a continent, as Missouri is, salt was a rare and important commodity. The natural existence of salt was good enough reason for a settlement to grow and the "harvest" of salt was an important occupation in early Missouri. Of course wildlife needed salt also so the presence of a salt lick meant an abundance of game. The many animals would lick the salty earth to get the salt and its "popularity" would usually cause the area to be trampled, muddy, and devoid of plant life. That's how the Boone family and others could usually identify the presence of salt.

Early centers of salt recovery were noted by Lewis and Clark and others in the area of Herculaneum and later at Boones Lick. Of course salt is found in Missouri place names like the Saline River, Knob Lick, Salt River, Salt River Hills, and Saline County. Down in Texas County there was what the locals called the Buffalo Lick and a town grew up near there. They called the new community "The Lick." In time, of course, it came to be called Licking.

The Osage were here for many years hunting and living alongside the white settlers. This and most settlement ended with the War Between the States which was especially hard on this area. After the war, whites began to return but the Osage didn't. A devastating tornado struck in 1880 and it took several years for the struggling community to rebuild. By 1889 there were three general stores and several specialty businesses. A good quality academy of learning was also there by 1889.

This little town in the big woods has any number of reasons for you to stop in today. One is the rodeo. The Professional Rodeo Cowboys Assn. has conducted a high-quality rodeo in Licking for over a quarter of a century. These are usually in early June. September brings an opportunity to visit the big three-story Licking Mill. The town showcases artists, crafters, and musicians in the mill.

While you're in the area, you can't help but notice the lumbering industry in operation. Licking has two pallet mills shipping thousands of pallets each week to places across the nation. They also have two charcoal companies producing thousands of tons of charcoal each year. You will no doubt see some of the thirty charcoal kilns that operate in the area.

The most surprising thing about Licking, Missouri is its Texas County Museum of Art and History. Can you imagine a small town like this having a museum with authentic signed works by Picasso, Charles Russell, Miro, or George Catlin? There are those and much more. This is only open on Mondays and Tuesdays from March to November. And, imagine this, it's free!

To this writer, the best thing in the Licking area is the upper Big Piney River. Folks in Kansas City and St. Louis are accustomed to seeing gigantic powerful rivers full of silt and logs. It's such a treat to experience places like the upper Meramec or the upper Big Piney where the water is clean, clear and cool even in the summertime. Stop for a while and get your feet wet. Put any kind of food on a string and catch some crawdads. This is truly too good to pass by.

Favorite Highways

Some highways are themselves worth the drive. Even if you're not going somewhere right on that highway, investing an extra thirty or forty minutes can improve your quality of life and your disposition. A good example is Highway 32 that runs from Ste. Genevieve, through Farmington, Park Hills, to Caledonia and its antiques. From there it continues through the Ozarks and Mark Twain National Forest to Licking, Plato, and Lebanon. Onward it goes to Bolivar, Stockton, and finally, El Dorado Springs.

The good part of this highway is the scenery, especially in the undeveloped Ozarks areas. It's a winding two-lane road all the way but it snakes past hills, forests, lakes, and freshwater streams. Did you notice how many of the communities above were also special enough to be included in this book? For many reasons, I know you will enjoy this drive

Missouri Highway 5 is the longest state highway we have. Since 1922 it has gone all the way from Missouri's southern border to the northern. From Arkansas it passes by Gainesville, and Ava to Mansfield. Then northward through Lebanon, the Lake of the Ozarks, Versailles, and Tipton. Then comes Boonville, Fayette, Walt Disney's home at Marceline, Gen. John Pershing's home at Laclede and northward across the tall grass prairie to Iowa.

Let's think about that route again. Starting with the beautiful Ozarks region of Ozark County and upward onto the Ozark Plateau, then continuing through the Lake region, through historic towns, and across the Missouri River Valley. Finally the last leg takes you across some of the richest farmland in the world.

Favorite Highways (cont.)

The American Automobile Assn. calls Highway 36 the Way of American Genius for good reason. Starting with St. Joseph you will think of milling and food giants along with the Pony Express. Going east on 36 brings you to J. C. Penney's hometown of Hamilton and Chillicothe where, for the first time in the history of the world, they figured a way to successfully market and sell sliced bread. Next we cross Laclede and Marceline (mentioned just above) and on to Hannibal which gave us the literary genius of Samuel Clemens. (Mark Twain)

Highway 50 runs from Maryland to California and in Missouri it has taken an important route since the days of stagecoaches. From St. Louis it passes through Union and the Missouri Wine Country to Jefferson City. Then westward through California, Sedalia, Warrensburg and Kansas City. Current discussions involve easing the traffic flow on Interstate 70 and this would force a widening and redirecting of much of Highway 50. To make this scenic and historic drive, you really should act soon.

If you're going either north or south across the state, consider using Highway 13 this time. Starting in the Mark Twain National Forest and crossing through Table Rock Lake country, you pass through pleasant small towns until you get to booming Springfield. Highway 13 is the Kansas Expressway through the Queen City of the Ozarks. Continuing northward across the Ozark Plateau you pass through Bolivar, Osceola, and the Truman Reservoir. Still a big divided highway, it takes you past impressive horse farms and a stop in Clinton or Warrensburg.

Favorite Highways (cont.)

Highway 21 takes you through some of our state's earliest and most historic places and then on to some of our most beautiful. From St. Louis it goes southward toward Potosi & Pilot Knob. But don't forget to stop at little Goldman and visit the Sandy Creek Covered Bridge. You will also want to spend some time and walk the grounds and the large redoubt remaining from the key Civil War battle at Pilot Knob. (Ironton) Make sure your gas tank is full because the rest of the journey to the Arkansas line will take you through miles and miles of very small towns and beautiful scenery in the Mark Twain National Forest area. You will finally reach a good-sized town at Doniphan. When I lived in the area I would try to plan my Highway 21 trips with the weather forecast in mind. This road is at its most amazing just after a good heavy rain. As you drive, the streams are running full and the bluffs along the road are sporting beautiful waterfalls. These wet weather occurrences are only there during and after rains.

Of course we know of **Highway 76** as the crowded main artery of Branson and Silver Dollar City. From there it continues through Cassville and terminates at the Oklahoma border in McDonald County. But east of Branson is a road that I love to Drive. From Taneyville on is a winding narrow little state highway (76) that runs north-eastward through Ava until it terminates at Willow Springs. There is really no reason to go this way except that, if you have an alternative, this one will show you scenery and refresh your tired outlook when compared to the other ways.

__Favorite Highways (cont.)__

Back to a two-lane road now and still further north, Higginsville has interesting Civil War sites as does your next stop, Lexington. Like Lexington, Richmond's southern heritage shows itself all over town. You will remember Gallatin from an earlier story and it is on Route 13. The road finally terminates near the Iowa border at Bethany. This road shows you the northern prairie and the southern flavor of this section of the Missouri River Valley. Then the lakes of central and south Missouri along with all the scenic vistas of the Ozarks.

In the state's earliest days a stagecoach road was needed between the first state capital and the permanent state capital. So Highway 94 was built along a trail from St. Charles to Jefferson City. It now runs from the Mississippi near the Alton Bridge to the north side of the Missouri opposite the state capital. This hilly winding road takes you smack through the middle of some of the most historic places in the state. You pass the history of St. Charles and the Weldon Springs area where much of the work was done to make our first atomic bombs. That place still has an eerie feel about it. The Busch Wildlife area is a paradise worth stopping for. Treat yourself to a short hike!

<u>Favorite Highways (cont.)</u>

Driving westward takes you through the heart of the Daniel Boone country and past the bluffs on the other side of the river where Meriwether Lewis fell over 200 feet before he "caught himself by his knife." The Labadie power plant also looms on that side of the river. Its smokestacks tower 700 feet into the air. As you near Augusta you become overwhelmed by the number of wineries and you can stop at any of them. They are all terrific. Just past Dutzow you have an opportunity to cross the river into Washington if you wish. Marthasville has some beautifully preserved log cabins if you want to take a look. And, of course Daniel and Rebecca Boone are buried there.

Continuing west on 94 you will come upon the prettiest little white country church to be seen anywhere. It's near Pinkney. People come to this church from across the nation for shape note singing. From this point onward there are no large towns until you get to Jefferson City. Just more and more of the hilly riverside roadway filled with beautiful scenery. In the fall you will need to plan on a little more time to travel anywhere on Highway 94 because of the wineries and the wonderful colorful leaves.

Favorite Highways (cont.)

US 54 runs from southwestern Missouri to the northeast. It is a major road through the Ozarks and takes you to Pomme de Terre Lake and Lake of the Ozarks. It goes through Nevada, El Dorado Springs, Hermitage, crosses the Lake of the Ozarks the first time just north of Ha Ha Tonka State Park, then passes through Camdenton. It crosses the lake a second time at Osage Beach before passing Eldon. It crosses the Missouri River at Jefferson City.

You will continue through Fulton, crossing Interstate 70 at Kingdom City, and on to Mexico, and Vandalia. You wind up at the Mississippi River in Louisiana. Recapping, this road leads you through some of our best history and across our biggest lake from the Ozarks to the Northern Prairie to the Big Muddy. What a trip!

The stretch of **Highway 19** between Mammoth Spring at Thayer and on up to Salem offers some of the best the state has to offer. Of course, there's the Mark Twain National Forest and then the area centered around Emminence gives us Alley Spring, Story's Creek School, Round Spring, Round Spring Cave, Big Spring, Blue Spring, Rocky Falls, Welch Spring, Akers Ferry, Pulltite Spring & Cabin, Jam Up Cave, Two Rivers and sections of the Ozark National Scenic Riverways! All this and I didn't even mention the grist mills.

<u>Favorite Highways (cont.)</u>

From Salem northward Highway 19 skirts the Indian Trails State Forest and the Mark Twain National Forest through the float tripping country around Steelville. Then, northward through Cuba, Owensville, across the Missouri at Hermann, and across the prairie to Montgomery City. Highway 19 continues on to New London just south of Hannibal. From our smallest rivers and springs to the two largest rivers on the continent and all of the scenery and history in between.

Trenton

Which city is America's largest producer of Vienna sausages? Yes, Trenton gets that honor! There are other things about Trenton that are interesting in their own ways and I'll try to mention a few. J. S. Lomax opened a general store on a bluff above the Grand River and a settlement grew up there and called itself "Lomax Store." Later they renamed the place Bluff Grove and were named as the county seat. In 1842 they chose their present name of Trenton. The surrounding area is known as the Green Hills.

As with many Missouri towns, growth was really spurred when the first railroad arrived. This convenience of transportation also caused the utopian Ruskin College to move to Trenton. This was followed by the college buying up the major businesses of Trenton and operating them on a co-op basis. I may be condensing this story too much but in 1903 the whole project came crashing down when the leader's wife divorced him and accused him of squandering $250,000 of her money.

It's interesting to note that Missouri has had at least five "utopias" during its history and they all have failed when they ran out of other people's money to spend. These are documented in my book *This Day in Missouri History*. The college itself moved from place to place but was completely extinct by 1919.

In 1925 the community established what is now North Central Missouri College and it continues to offer a fine program especially in agriculture and nursing. Trenton remembers famous visitors like Herbert Hoover and Jesse Owens who have spent time here. However, One of the events that shaped Trenton's history and personality was a very sad one.

The Rock Island Railroad operated a repairs facility here called the Roundhouse. In the 1940s they had a lot of labor problems which resulted in a bitter strike. At one point the strikers beat a replacement worker to death. The town chose to take no action and no one was prosecuted or punished. The railroad closed the Roundhouse and Trenton's population has been declining ever since.

That was three generations ago and Trenton is a peaceful farming community now and welcoming to all visitors. The county Historical Society operates three facilities which together make up the Grundy County Museum. This museum is a pleasant surprise in the quality of its collection. Nothing spectacular – just a good reflection of the way things used to be.

I suggest visiting in mid to late October when they are celebrating Missouri Days. This brings lots of small-town, down-home fun with coloring contests, yard decorating contests, a baby show, parades, community church service, an FFA petting zoo, and more. One day features a full day of band competitions. Missouri Days parades may have more than fifty marching bands!

I suggest that you go to both the sponsored soup supper and the pancake and sausage breakfast for your meals and camaraderie. My visit requires the community church service then a stroll through the vendors, and the Rollin' Relics Car Show. How about you?

Glasgow

Glasgow is the kind of town that's proud of having Missouri's oldest family-owned pharmacy. It brags about its family-owned restaurants and scoffs at other places with their franchise eateries. Glasgow has the oldest bank in Missouri and it rightly feels pride in having the oldest public library in its original building anywhere west of the Mississippi. At one time it was a booming river town shipping hemp and tobacco from the local farms. It's still a booming river town, but now shipping corn from the local farms. I'm sure they could change and become more ordinary but I'm glad they haven't.

I appreciate the attitude of a town that's proud of its schools. Especially when, instead of bragging about just the sports teams, they brag about the basketball championships and the academic competitions.

A while back, one resident told me to drive across the new bridge. "You won't hardly know you're on a bridge," he said. It is the modern style with no superstructure and it replaced a very historic one. The original bridge was the first non-toll bridge across the Missouri and it was the world's first multiple-span all-steel bridge. Because of its place in history some folks resent the loss of the old bridge. Having driven across it many times, I am appreciative of the new modern one.

Two of my favorite events from Glasgow's history are: from a time when the northern Colonel, Benjamin Lewis offered a $6,000 reward for William (Bloody Bill) Anderson. Upon hearing Lewis had $6,000, Anderson went to Glasgow and demanded the money for himself. Oops! Lewis suffered greatly for not thinking that one all the way through. The other of my favorite events happened when Glasgow's great barnstorming pitcher, John Donaldson, gained recognition for baseball abilities. It was early in the 20th century and African-Americans weren't yet playing in the majors. Tug McGraw of the New York Giants, offered a spectacular $50,000 contract if Donaldson would go to Cuba and play ball there. McGraw planned to draft Donaldson from Cuba and let him play for the Giants. The indignant John Donaldson, refusing to take part in the lie, said he wouldn't renounce his family or his race.

Glasgow is so close to so many important places in Missouri that everyone is likely to be near Glasgow some time. If it's been a while since you took the time to visit this pleasant place with its beautiful antebellum homes, you owe it to yourself to spend a little time here.

St. Paul's, Concordia

This city is proud of St. Paul Lutheran High School—the only residential high school affiliated with the Lutheran Church-Missouri Synod in the United States and the second-oldest Lutheran high school in the nation. The story of the school may not fit the nature of this book but it is a wonderful story just the same. You may remember when, earlier in the book, I spoke of the German immigrants who settled along the Mississippi River and founded a school which became the Concordia Seminary of the Lutheran Church – Missouri Synod.

One of the five little boys attending that first school was Julius Biltz, a 13-year old orphan. He had hidden himself aboard a ship bound for the New World and succeeded in his journey to Missouri. I'm not doing justice to his wonderful story but he grew and was educated so that he could become a clergyman. He went to a new town in the west and named the place Concordia. He then started a school which he called St. Paul's, the same name as the local church.

When you drive through Concordia, MO today, you will definitely notice St. Paul's. It is a landmark which has sent many young men into the service of the Lutheran Church as it spread across the young America.

Caruthersville

Caruthersville is the county seat for Pemiscot County. The word "Pemiscot" is an American Indian word meaning "liquid mud" and it must have been very fitting in the old days. This low area next to the Mississippi was the home to Mound Builders in its pre-history and then sparse settlement afterwards. It was just too marshy and mosquito-ridden to attract a large population. Then in 1857 John Hardeman Walker and George W. Bushey laid out the town.

When Missouri applied for statehood, it was Walker who pushed to have Lapland included in our state. We call this area the Bootheel but some residents call it Lapland because it "laps" over into Arkansas. The result is that we have one part of our state which is different from all other parts. John Hardeman Walker was a very interesting character and, if you like, you can read more about him in *Tales From Missouri and the Heartland.*

A big event occurred in 1893 when the state's legislature created the Saint Francis Levee District. This act authorized taxes for the purpose of building, repairing, protecting and maintaining levees in the district. All of a sudden the area was seen as being much safer from flooding and Sterling Price Reynolds worked to create a series of drainage ditches which meant that excess water would run off the land thus creating workable rich farmland and eliminating the disease-carrying mosquitoes which had plagued the area.

In 1976 a new bridge was opened across the Mississippi River which made Caruthersville an important transportation link for the area. Mississippi barge traffic is now an important part of the city's economy. Of course this is an important part of the farm-to-market process for area farmers.

April 2, 2006 was a terrible night for Caruthersville. Over 60% of the town was destroyed by a string of tornadoes. 1,500 people were left homeless after the storm and many were injured. Somehow, no one in the town was killed. Rebuilding the schools, homes, and businesses was a terrible problem but the local folks were up to the challenge.

A Missourian visiting Caruthersville from any other part of the state should do so with an eye to the uniqueness of the place. It is so different from other sections! The striking vision of truly flat land may be the first thing to grab your attention. This is especially true at night when the farm lights stretch out and look for all the world like ships at sea. A solitary Indian mound may surprise you. The series of straight drainage canals stretching to the horizon is something you won't see in your home county. The gigantic strings of barges moving in and past the Caruthersville port is different but maybe the main difference is the farm crops.

Where else in the state do you find rice and cotton as two of the main crops? This rich, flat land with an abundance of water is perfect for those crops. By the way, much of the rice goes straight up the river to the Anheuser-Busch Brewery in St. Louis. These crops provide two interesting things for visitors. One is those great little spray planes doing acrobatic flying as the dust the crops with insecticides. The other is best seen in the late summer and fall.

Cotton is picked, transported, and stored, and processed by huge machines not seen in areas outside the Bootheel. During and after the harvest, stray cotton bolls blow across the roads like warm-weather snow. Elongated straight mountains of cotton line the roads waiting their turn to be processed or shipped. It's an experience just to be here and drink it in. I can't leave the subject of attractions in the area without mentioning the casino which pumped some badly-needed tourist revenue back into the local economy after the tornadoes.

In addition to some old-time characters like John Hardemann Walker Caruthersville has given us some modern people of note. John B. England, Missouri's great fighter ace in World War II was a native of Caruthersville. In 2004 Cedric the Entertainer featured his home town in a movie. In the film, *Johnson Family Vacation*, he journeys from California to a reunion of his family in Caruthersville.

This writer's favorite Missouri artist, Gary Lucy, is a Caruthersville native. Knowing this, helps to explain why he paints such stirring historic portrayals of life on Missouri's rivers. When you visit Caruthersville and Pemiscot County, try to do it with an artist's eye for this place. It is so different from your Missouri home that it deserves a long close look.

FIND IT!

QUICK & EASY

Match the numbered regions below with the names on the following pages and plan some great day trips and excursions to places   too good to pass by.

Match these names with the regions shown on the previous page.

Missouri Place of Interest	Found in Zone	Page Number
Akers Ferry	7	280
Alley Spring Mill	7	232
Arrow Rock	4	149
Ash Grove	6	107
Augusta	4 on the edge of 5	299
Ball of Human Hair	5	173
Ball of String	1	173
Banjo	7	173
Big Oak Tree	7	135
Blackwater	4	37
Boat Henge	4	89
Bob's Gasoline Alley	4 on the edge of 5	259
Bollinger Mill	8	233
Boone Graves	5	55

California	4	209
Canton Ferry	2	281
Carthage	6	201
Caruthersville	8	353
Caveman Barbeque	7	96
Clarksville	(**junction of 2, 4, & 5**)	237
Clinton	3	301
Concordia (St. Paul's)	3	351
Crane's Country Store	4	129
Cuba Murals	4	93
Dawt Mill	7	231
Defiance	5	265
De Soto	5	249
Devil's Elbow	7	7
Dillard Mill	7	233
Dorena-Hickman Ferry	8	282
Dutzow	4	51
Edwards Mill	7	234
El Dorado Springs	6	313
Excelsior Springs	3	253

Falling Spring Mill	7	233
Fire Fighters Memorial	4	80
Florissant	5	227
Fork (35 feet tall)	7	176
Fort Davidson	8	83
Ft. Leonard. Wood (Military Museum)	7	157
Fort Osage	3	205
Frankenstein	4	131
Fredericksburg Ferry	4	279
Frohna	8	311
Fulton	4	215
Galena	**6 on the edge of 7**	307
Gallatin	**1**	**13**
Gerald Roller Mill	**4 at the edge of 5**	235
Giant Chigger	2	173
Giant Frog	7	174
Giant Goose (Maxie)	2	171
Giant Mushroom	6	173
Giant Pecan	2	172

Giant Pacifier	4	173
Glasgow	4	349
Golden Eagle Ferry	5	280
Grand Falls	6	97
Hamilton	1	183
Hammond Mill	7	231
Hands in Prayer	6	173
Hannibal	2	283
Heartland Dairies	2	287
Herculaneum	5	321
Hermann	4	153
Hodgson Mill	8	232
Hornersville	8	165
Ilasco	2	239
Kimmswick	5	193
Knob Noster	3	245
Labadie	5	77
Lebanon	7	123
Lexington	3	101
Licking	7	335

Lost Valley Hatchery	**3 on the edge of 4**	133
Louisiana	2	317
McDonald County	6	145
Mansfield	7	289
Marionville: White Squirrels	6	86
Marshall	4	293
Marshfield	7	23
Mastodons	5	199
Maxie the Goose	2	171
Meramec Caverns	4	84
Milnot Can	6	173
Milan	2	213
Monett	6	47
Montauk Mill	7	234
Neosho	6	139
Nevada	6	325
New Haven	4	295
Old Drum *Warrensburg*	3	137
Old Mines	**5 on the edge of 8**	99

Osceola	**3 on the edge of 6**	1
Overland	5	221
Patton	8	223
Pete Kibble's Foot	2	213
Pink Ice Cream Cone	1	173
Plato	7	157
Potosi	8	41
Pumpkin Festival	4	90
Puxico Library	8	94
Ralph Foster Museum	7	92
Reed Spring Mill	**7 on the edge of 8**	232
River's Edge	4	132
Rocheport	4	19
Rockbridge Mill	7	232
Rocking Chair (Four Stories Tall)	**4 on the edge of 7**	176
St. Charles	5	255
Ste. Genevieve	**5 on the edge of 8**	261
Ste. Genevieve: Madoc Ferry	**5 on the edge of 8**	281

Saint Mary	8	315
Sandy Creek Bridge	5	134
Steelville	7	61
Stars & Stripes Museum	8	87
Tipton	4	329
Topaz Mill	7	233
Towosahgy	8	136
Trenton	1 on the edge of 2	345
Vibernum	7	333
The Village *Unity Village*	3	169
Vintage Base Ball *St Louis*	5	269
Washington	4	65
Watkins Woolen Mill *Lawson*	1	234
Waynesville (O.S.S.& Croaker)	7	95
Weingarten	7	33
Weston	1	57
Whiteman Air Force Base *Knob Noster*	3 on the edge of 4	246
Williamsburg	4	129
Zanoni Mill	7	232

Giant Teeth	5	**175**
Giant Turtle	5	**175**
Giant's Head	5	**175**
Laumeier Sculpture Park	5	**29**
Missouri Botanical Gardens	5	**29**
Missouri History Museum	5	**28**
Municipal Opera	5	**28**
Vintage Base Ball (Lafayette Park)	5	**269**
The Wabash, Frisco, and Pacific Railroad	5	**226**

Cautionary Note and Suggestion

As I speak to folks across the state, people often ask, "How do you know all of this?" The principal reason is that I taught Missouri Studies for many years.

Of course another reason is that I'm fascinated by our state and its stories. For our entire history, Missouri's students have been learning about what makes their state and their locality unique. That is, after all, their heritage.

Now there is a headlong rush for accountability in the schools and that is something to be applauded. However, the zeal for accountability has led some shallow thinkers to demand nationally standardized testing for every subject at every grade level. This could be disastrous.

How can you create a nationally standardized test for a state's history, let alone local history? Of course you can't!

Missouri's history is very different from that of Hawaii. The history of Vermont has little in common with the history of California, Washington, or Louisiana. The Common Core and other programs may have sprung from good intentions but they must not be allowed to morph into some national monster that robs us of our heritage.

Some of the same people who challenge us to celebrate diversity are seen to be backing these educational programs that hold the possibility of belittling and destroying America's diversity.

The very people who read books like this are the ones who must stand up for the appreciation and continuation of our state's history and geography curriculum. That would be you.

Well, that was the cautionary note. Now for the suggestion. Why not invite this writer to speak about our unique state at your organization's next meeting?

I have several topics and even a game about traveling around the state in your car. If you're interested, or if you would like to contribute a fact or an idea for the next edition, just send me a note at:

RnDMalone@att.net

If you might like to see more books about Missouri, visit my Author's Page on Amazon.com. Thank you for your interest!

Ross W. Malone